Abu Dhabi
Garden City of the Gulf

Peter Hellyer and Ian Fairservice

Published by Motivate Publishing

Dubai: PO Box 2331, Dubai, UAE
Tel: (+971 4) 282 4060; fax: (+971 4) 282 7898
e-mail: books@motivate.ae   www.booksarabia.com

Office 508, Building No 8, Dubai Media City, Dubai, UAE
Tel: (+971 4) 390 3550; fax: (+971 4) 390 4845

Abu Dhabi: PO Box 43072, Abu Dhabi, UAE
Tel: (+971 2) 677 2005; fax: (+971 2) 677 0124

London: Acre House, 11/15 William Road, London NW1 3ER
e-mail: motivateuk@motivate.ae

Directors:	Obaid Humaid Al Tayer
	Ian Fairservice
Consultant Editor:	David Steele
Editors:	Albert Harvey Pincis
	Moushumi Nandy
Assistant Editor:	Zelda Pinto
Art Director:	Andrea Willmore
Senior Designer:	Cithadel Francisco
Designer:	Charlie Banalo

General Manager Books: Jonathan Griffiths

First published 1988
Second edition 1990
Third edition 1992
Reprinted 1994, 1995
Fourth edition 1999
Fifth edition 2003
Sixth edition 2008

© Motivate Publishing

All rights reserved. No part of this publication may be reproduced in any material form (including photocopying or storing in any medium by electronic means) without the written permission of the copyright holders. Applications for the copyright holders' written permission to reproduce any part of this publication should be addressed to the publishers. In accordance with the International Copyright Act 1956 and the UAE Federal Law No. (7) of 2002, Concerning Copyrights and Neighboring Rights, any person acting in contravention of this will be liable to criminal prosecution and civil claims for damages.

ISBN: 978 1 86063 192 4

British Library Cataloguing-in-Publication Data. A catalogue record for this book is available from the British Library.

Printed by Rashid Printers & Stationers LLC, Ajman, UAE

Photographic Credits

Abu Dhabi Airports Company: 49
Abu Dhabi Duty Free: 92/93
ADCO: 24T, 24B, 28
ADNOC: 52, 53
Ali, Mohammad Arfan: 64
Arabian Eye: 8, 9
Codrai, Ronald: 50
Gallo Images/Getty Images: 20, 21, 22, 23, 27, 39, 44/45

Hellyer, Peter: 54
Gulfpics: 19
  Newington, Greg: 4, 6/7, 11, 12, 14, 40, 83
  Salik, Farooq: 42
  Shankar, Adisehan: 66, 67, 78
  Walsh, Callaghan: 1, 88
Rashid, Noor Ali: 29
Steele, David: Front cover, back

cover, 10, 13, 17, 18, 30, 31, 35, 36, 47, 60, 61, 63, 65, 68, 69, 70/71, 72, 73, 77, 86, 87, 91
Sunshine Tours: 74, 75
TotalFinaElf: 51
Victory Team: 76
Willmore, Andrea: 32
Zandi, Dariush: 56, 84w

His Highness, Sheikh Khalifa bin Zayed Al Nahyan, President of the United Arab Emirates and Ruler of Abu Dhabi.

Foreword

By Sheikh Nahayan bin Mabarak Al Nahayan

It is my pleasure to introduce this new and updated edition of *Abu Dhabi – Garden City of the Gulf*.

Like its previous versions, this book presents an interesting portrait of the city of Abu Dhabi. It is a story of the place and its people that captures the important features of the city's development, history, character and achievements.

We are very proud of the advances that Abu Dhabi continues to make in all spheres of life. Our city is one of the world's best places to live and work. It is also an excellent place for business and commerce.

Our greatest fortune in Abu Dhabi has been that the leaders of our country are people of wisdom and vision. We are extremely fortunate that Sheikh Zayed bin Sultan Al Nahyan was our founding President. Sheikh Zayed was a man of peace and progress. He was able to see beyond the horizon and chart a path for our country's future. He led the building of our country as a place that welcomes people from round the world, a place of harmony and safety, and a land where we see lush greenery where once there was only desert. Sheikh Zayed led the creation of the physical infrastructure that ensures for our citizens modern conveniences – roads, schools, hospitals, airports and telecommunications. Just as important, he led the creation of our social infrastructure that values knowledge, peace and global understanding. The wise and strong leadership of Sheikh Zayed made Abu Dhabi and the United Arab Emirates places of progress, prosperity and stability.

We are fortunate, as well, that after Sheikh Zayed's passing, the leadership of our country passed to His Highness Sheikh Khalifa bin Zayed Al Nahyan, who shares the values of his father and continues his vision. And, especially pertinent to this publication, we also have the able leadership of His Highness Sheikh Mohammed bin Zayed Al Nahyan, Crown Prince of Abu Dhabi and Deputy Supreme Commander of the Armed Forces. Under the enlightened leadership of both Sheikh Khalifa and Sheikh Mohammed, Abu Dhabi is moving forward with deliberate strategies for the future. Under their leadership, Abu Dhabi is committed to creating a knowledge society, to boosting creativity and innovation, and to learning from successful experiences round the globe. As we watch Abu Dhabi grow into one of the important global cultural and economic centres, we all share in the keen awareness of what this wonderful city has come to represent in its unique blend of modernity, history and heritage.

I take this opportunity to reiterate my strong belief that if our past, our heritage and our present are any indication of our future, Abu Dhabi will continue to reflect the unique spirit and character that has guided its development over the years. All of us who live and work in Abu Dhabi are proud to be part of that spirit and to embody that character.

Nahayan Mabarak Al Nahayan
Minister of Higher Education and Scientific Research
United Arab Emirates

Front cover: Abu Dhabi, the 'Garden City of the Gulf', has some 20 well-maintained parks.

Title page: Modern Abu Dhabi is a cosmopolitan, high-rise city, but its foundations are firmly rooted in the Islamic faith.

Opposite page: Traditional fishing dhows moored in the Dhow Harbour east of Abu Dhabi Corniche.

Following spread: The Al Maqta'a Bridge links the island of Abu Dhabi with its hinterland. The old watchtower previously guarded a causeway at the same point.

Contents

The United Arab Emirates	8
Ruler and President	20
The Land, its Heritage and People	30
A Thriving Economy	39
The Oil-and-Gas Sector	50
A Green and Pleasant Emirate	63
Abu Dhabi's Leisure Industry	74
The World on Display	86

Abu Dhabi – Garden City of the Gulf

Chapter One
The United Arab Emirates

Sheikh Zayed bin Sultan Al Nahyan signs the Federation Agreement on 2 December 1971, giving birth to the United Arab Emirates. On his left is Sheikh Rashid bin Saeed Al Maktoum and behind them are Mehdi Al Tajir, Sheikh Maktoum bin Rashid Al Maktoum and Sheikh Hamdan bin Rashid Al Maktoum.

In March 1968, the rulers of seven sheikhdoms known as the Trucial States, on the south-eastern flank of the Arabian Peninsula, came together to form a federation. In the nature of such moves, it took a little while before the structure of the new state was finally agreed, but on 2 December 1971 a new country, the United Arab Emirates (UAE), took its place on the international stage.

Emerging after a British presence in the region that had lasted a century and a half, the seven were disparate in size, population and resources, the smallest, Ajman, being a mere 259 square kilometres and the largest, Abu Dhabi, about 80,000 square kilometres. The total population in 1968 was only around 180,000, and much of the country had no roads, no schools, no hospitals, and little in the way of a modern developed infrastructure, even though the discovery of oil a few years earlier held out the hope of better things to come.

The seven rulers, led by Sheikh Zayed bin Sultan Al Nahyan, Ruler of the largest of the sheikhdoms, Abu Dhabi, felt that they had little option but to agree to form

The United Arab Emirates

their federation, for the British had made it clear that nothing would delay their departure at the end of 1971. With varying degrees of enthusiasm and confidence, the new state and its leaders set out to face the challenges of the future.

Many outside observers, citing poverty, history and the often tempestuous seas of Middle East politics, gave the new state little chance of success. As is so often the case, however, the foretellers of doom were proven wrong. In the years that have followed, the United Arab Emirates has undergone a rapid process of economic development and social change that has occurred against a backdrop of an enviable internal stability, despite the impact of two major wars and revolution in the region. This transformation has been assisted by a mass immigration of expatriate workers that has seen the total population climb to nearly four and a half million.

The citizens of the UAE, which comprises the Emirates of Abu Dhabi, Dubai, Sharjah, Ra's al-Khaimah, Fujairah, Umm al-Qaiwain and Ajman, have seen their

Under the new flag of the United Arab Emirates are, from left: Sheikh Khalid bin Mohammed Al Qasimi, Sheikh Rashid bin Saeed Al Maktoum, Sheikh Zayed bin Sultan, Sheikh Rashid bin Humaid Al Nuaimi, Sheikh Mohammed bin Hamad Al Sharqi and Sheikh Rashid bin Ahmed Al Mualla.

Abu Dhabi – Garden City of the Gulf

A dramatic view of the rugged Hajar Mountains, the main chain of mountains of the United Arab Emirates and the backbone of Arabia.

lives change completely within the space of a generation. Indeed, more than half of the country's citizens have been born since 1971, and have known nothing else but federation.

The speed of the transformation, and the way in which it has been absorbed, is particularly remarkable because the lifestyle of the people, in what is now the Emirates, had remained almost unchanged for hundreds, perhaps thousands of years – a life of unrelenting struggle to live in one of the world's most unyielding environments.

The old ways involved survival in the heat of summer in one of the most austere deserts on earth, on the edge of the Rub al-Khali (The Empty Quarter), or in the Hajar Mountains, where a brief respite during winter rains was soon forgotten amid the baked and barren rocks. Survival, on land at least, was a matter of pastoral nomadism or scratching a living from small agricultural plots; the sea offered more in the way of resources, such as the world-famous pearls of the Gulf, but collecting them was a task to test even the most hardy.

Yet against this most uncompromising of backgrounds, the people of the Emirates have managed to survive, winning for their country an important place on the map of international maritime commerce, with Emirati sailors venturing to East Africa and China as far back as 2,000 years ago.

Today, the UAE is one of the world's top oil producers and, thanks to the wealth from oil and gas production and, more importantly, to the way in which the country's leaders have utilized that wealth for the benefit of the people, the hardships of the past are a fading memory. While the people of the UAE continue to derive much of the strength of their society from the heritage of a difficult past, they are now able, with confidence, to look forward to a prosperous future.

Abu Dhabi

The Emirate of Abu Dhabi, which has provided the overwhelming bulk of the funds that have paid for the federation's development, is by far the largest of the

The United Arab Emirates

Glass-clad skyscrapers provide a unique backdrop to the ubiquitous date palms in one of the many pleasant parks in the city of Abu Dhabi.

seven emirates, with an area of 80,000 square kilometres, 17 times larger than the second Emirate of Dubai, and amounting to more than 86 per cent of the total area of the federation.

It has the largest population, 1.7 million out of a total of 4.32 million, according to the latest census, and also has the lion's share of the UAE's oil and gas resources. Though producing around 2.7-million barrels a day in early 2007, it has plans to increase capacity to around 3.5-million barrels a day by 2010 and eventually to around four million. It also has sufficient reserves for more than 100 years at present production rates, as well as the world's fourth-largest reserves of natural gas.

Once a major power in south-eastern Arabia (see 'The Land, its Heritage and People'), Abu Dhabi fell upon hard times in the 1930s and 1940s, partially as a result of the international economic depression and the Second World War that followed, and partially because of the introduction of the Japanese cultured pearl, which destroyed the market for Abu Dhabi's most prized export – the pure, natural Gulf pearl.

Ironically, oil, the source of the economic miracle that has since changed the face of Abu Dhabi and the other emirates, was also first produced from beneath the sea – or rather the seabed.

Oil exploration in Abu Dhabi commenced in the late 1940s, although the first oil well, drilled at Ra's Sadr, north-east of Abu Dhabi, in 1950, was a dry hole. It was not until the late 1950s that commercially viable oil deposits were found, first offshore, at Umm Shaif, then onshore, at Bab. Exports commenced in 1962 and Abu Dhabi entered the oil era.

In 1966, a few years later, Sheikh Zayed became the Ruler of the Emirate and the process of development got fully under way. In the years that have passed since then, the Emirate has been transformed, and, thanks to the generosity of Sheikh Zayed, and, since his death in 2004, of his successor, His Highness Sheikh Khalifa bin Zayed Al Nahyan, now also the UAE's President, its oil and gas

Abu Dhabi – Garden City of the Gulf

revenues have also underpinned development elsewhere in the country.

The city of Abu Dhabi has, naturally, attracted a large proportion of the development expenditure, some of the results of which can be seen in the pages that follow. At the time that the production of oil began, it was little more than a coastal village and one which, moreover, appeared to have changed little in centuries, thanks to the economic slump that followed the collapse of the pearling industry.

A comparison between pictures from that time and those of the city today show clearly the extent of the remarkable change that has taken place. Amid the skyscrapers and broad thoroughfares of the city today only three buildings from the past survive, one a simple watchtower that still stands like a sentinel at the approaches to the island, and another Qasr al-Hosn, the old fort and former ancestral home of the ruling Al Nahyan family, before becoming the government's Centre for Documentation and Research and now destined to become a showpiece museum of the recent past.

Abu Dhabi for many years appeared to lack some of the commercial verve of its neighbour Dubai, although that has changed markedly in recent years, but it has had the advantage not only of its oil and gas revenues but also of massive financial reserves.

In recent years, a move towards the privatization of key sectors of the state-owned economy has been coupled with an innovative offsets programme that requires companies winning major military contracts to invest part of the proceeds in productive industrial ventures; and, since 2005, the launching of a massive investment programme, both from the government and from the private sector, in residential property development, new industries and expansion of facilities such as hotels and a new airport, as well as a major initiative to make

Qasr al-Hosn – also known as The White Fort – is destined to become a showpiece museum and the cultural heart of the nation.

The United Arab Emirates

the city an international cultural capital. Building on the basis established in the first four decades of oil production, a new phase of expansion is now getting under way.

At the same time, its dozens of parks, gardens and well-planted roadsides have given the city a green image that has, with justification, earned it the nickname of 'Garden City of the Gulf.'

The Emirate of Abu Dhabi is, however, much more than just the city itself. Roughly 160 kilometres east of the city lies its inland counterpart of Al Ain (itself the subject of another book in the Arabian Heritage Series: *Al Ain – Oasis City*). A conurbation of nearly 400,000 people, Al Ain is the heart of the Emirate's agricultural region, with farms and palm groves yielding tens of thousands of tonnes of produce a year, continuing an agricultural tradition that stretches back at least to the early Bronze Age, more than 5,000 years ago.

South-west of Abu Dhabi is the Liwa Oasis, an arc of oases more than 50 kilometres in length on the very edge of the Empty Quarter that is the traditional home of the Bani Yas tribal confederation, today headed by President Sheikh Khalifa. To the north of Liwa is the burgeoning township of Medinat (Bida) Zayed, capital of the Emirate's Western Region, which provides a good centre for touring the surrounding deserts, although the inexperienced should always take care when driving off-road.

The Emirate's coast begins at Ghantoot, in the north-east, running south-west past the huge Taweela power and water-desalination plant, with the site for the new Khalifa Port and Industrial Zone nearby, and a sheltered system of lagoons and inshore islands (some now the sites for new residential property developments), that stretch to the capital, Abu Dhabi, itself also on an island, though with suburbs rapidly developing on the adjacent mainland.

Attab Fort, between the village of Hmeem and the town of Meziyrah, is a fine example of the recently renovated forts in the Liwa Crescent.

Abu Dhabi – Garden City of the Gulf

To the west of the capital city lie more lagoons, islands and rocky headlands that stretch beyond the growing town of Mirfa, as far as the industrial complex of Ruwais and Jebel Dhanna, now an important centre for petrochemicals and oil refining, as well as the main onshore oil export terminal. Beyond is the vast expanse of the Sabkhat Matti, one of the largest salt flats in the world, with the barren and rocky Sila'a Peninsula on its western edge, this being followed by a stretch of coastline that extends round to the southern tip of the Qatar Peninsula.

A fine highway runs just inland from the coast all the way from Ghantoot to Sila'a, a distance of more than 400 kilometres, and then on to Khor al-Udaid, with smaller roads or well-graded tracks permitting easy access to the coast at several points.

Much more difficult to reach, however, are the Emirate's many islands. Some are little more than sandbanks, which may help to account for the fact that estimates of their number vary widely, but there are certainly more than a hundred. Among the most important, apart from Abu Dhabi itself, are Abu al-Abyadh, the largest; Sir Bani Yas, a nature reserve first established by President Sheikh Zayed and now scheduled to become a major tourist resort; Dalma, a centre of the fishing and pearling industry for thousands of years; Marawah, also with important archaeological sites, including the oldest village yet found in the Emirates, dating back to around 5500 BC; Qarnein, with breeding sea-bird colonies of international importance; and the oil-industry islands of Das, Zirku and Arzanah.

The variety of the geography and scenery will astound most visitors, but then the Emirate of Abu Dhabi, with its mixture of modern development and traditional heritage, is in many ways a remarkable place.

Dubai grew up along the banks of the Creek. The placid waterway is still considered as the heart of the city known as the 'Gateway to the Gulf'.

Dubai

Second largest of the seven emirates, Dubai has an area of some 4,000 square kilometres facing on to the Arabian Gulf Coast with a desert hinterland and a small enclave at Hatta, on the road east through the Hajar Mountains to Oman's port of Sohar. Proud of its title of 'Gateway to the Gulf' and its status as the uncontested commercial capital of the country, it has a history stretching back more than 4,000 years. The latest estimates put the population at 1.29 million, nearly all of whom live in the twin towns of Bur Dubai and Deira and their adjacent suburbs, including Jumeirah and the rapidly expanding Jebel Ali, the largest conurbation in the Emirates.

Dubai's Ruler is HH Sheikh Mohammed bin Rashid Al Maktoum, also the UAE's Vice-President and Prime Minister, who succeeded his elder brother, Sheikh Maktoum, at the beginning of 2006. Dubai has a long heritage of trade astride the country's longest and deepest *khor* (creek), stretching back for at least 3,000 years, and has built upon this to emerge as the country's commercial centre. With its ports of Port Rashid, in the city, and Jebel Ali, on the western edge, it handles nearly two thirds of the country's total imports, while an array of hotels and shopping and sports facilities has also contributed to its emergence as the top holiday destination for visitors in the Arabian Gulf.

Although an oil producer, Dubai has relatively small reserves and has for many years recognized the need to diversify its economy in preparation for the day when the oil runs out, some time early this century.

The diversification programme has achieved remarkable results. A world-class array of services has attracted hundreds of regional and international firms that now use the city as their Middle East base. The port of Jebel Ali, the largest man-made port in the world, is home to the region's largest Free Trade Zone, where considerably more than a billion US dollars have been invested, and from where products are exported throughout the area. The requirement for a heavy industrial base has been met by companies such as the DUBAL aluminium smelter and the DUCAB cable plant, while assembly and manufacturing plants range from cars to computers.

In the late 1990s, the focus turned to hi-tech industry, and the successful launching of the Dubai Internet City and the Dubai Media City has made the city a regional leader in modern communications and media technology. The latest phase of development has included massive residential property developments, both onshore, such as Burj Dubai, the world's tallest building, and on artificially created islands offshore, that are set to more than double Dubai's population during the next few years. These, together with a planned second airport, Al Maktoum International Airport, at Jebel Ali, which will be the largest in the world, and leisure facilities such as Dubailand, should help to reinforce Dubai's position as one of the world's fastest-growing tourist destinations. Another developing area of activity is banking and finance, with the Dubai International Finance Centre emerging as an important global player.

An array of superb hotels offers a tempting choice of services for visitors, whether bent on business or pleasure; while top international sporting events such as the Dubai Desert Classic (golf), the Dubai World Cup (horse-racing) and the Dubai Duty Free Open Tennis Tournament, compete with other events, including offshore power-boat racing, to attract the crowds.

Also home to one of the world's most successful airlines, Emirates, the city is now able to attract many millions of visitors a year to events such as the annual Dubai Shopping Festival and the Dubai Summer Surprises. Cosmopolitan and free-wheeling in its approach to business, Dubai has successfully drawn on its commercial heritage to plan for the future, and seems certain to continue to do so in the years ahead.

Sharjah and the Northern Emirates

Stretching along the Arabian Gulf coast north-east of Dubai and away across the Hajar Mountains to the Gulf of Oman on the other side are the remaining five emirates.

The largest of these is Sharjah, with an area of some 2,600 square kilometres and a population of around 680,000. The city of Sharjah itself, a few kilometres north of Dubai, is the seat of the ruling Al Qasimi family, descendants of the sheikhs who battled the British for control of the waterways of the Arabian Gulf at the beginning of the 19th century. A branch of the family also rules the northernmost Emirate of Ra's al-Khaimah. Sharjah Emirate stretches inland to the oasis of Dhaid, in the lee of the Hajar Mountains, while there are three enclaves, Kalba, Khor Fakkan and Dibba al-Husn, on the country's Gulf of Oman coast.

Some of the Emirate's ancient heritage can be found in the finely restored old forts and buildings to be seen, for example, in the old district of Sharjah and in Kalba, while there are also a number of major archaeological sites. Tell Abraq, north of Sharjah, is a tell (or settlement mound) dating back more than 4,000 years, while Muwailah, an Iron Age village near Sharjah Airport, has yielded the oldest writing ever found in the UAE, dating to the local Iron Age. At Jebel Buhays, south of Dhaid, archaeologists have found a Late Stone Age cemetery, more than 6,000 years old, with a mass grave of more than 400 people, and, nearby, evidence of occupation in Palaeolithic times, some 100,000 years ago.

Sharjah prides itself on its cultural traditions. Indeed the city was named by UNESCO as Arab Cultural Capital for 1998, an honour much prized by the Ruler, HH Dr Sheikh Sultan bin Mohammed Al Qasimi, himself an historian of note. With several museums, an impressive cultural centre, Islamic-style architecture, two universities, the country's largest annual book fair and a lively tradition of art and theatre, the Emirate also lays uncontested claim to being the cultural capital of the UAE.

It is at the same time rapidly developing a widely diversified economy. Oil and gas revenues from the offshore Mubarak field, and the Saja'a, Moveyeid and Kahaif fields, onshore, have helped to underpin an industrial sector that focuses on the light-manufacturing industry.

The east coast port of Khor Fakkan is one of the UAE's top container terminals, capitalizing on its strategic location outside the Strait of Hormuz. The port of Hamriyyah, on the Arabian Gulf coast, is now an important terminal for the export of liquefied natural gas and condensate from the onshore oilfields. The adjacent free zone is is also expanding rapidly.

Adjacent to the city of Sharjah is Ajman, smallest of the emirates and completely surrounded by Sharjah, apart from two tiny mountain enclaves at Manama and Masfut. Just 259 square kilometres in size, its population in the last census was around 251,000, many of whom work in nearby Sharjah and Dubai but have been attracted by Ajman's competitive accommodation costs and less frenetic pace of life.

Deriving much of its income from the provision of services, Ajman has no commercially viable deposits of hydrocarbons, but has successfully established one of the UAE's major heavy industrial ventures, the Arab Heavy Industries Shipyard, close to one of the UAE's major dhow-building yards. This offers visitors an interesting comparison of traditional and modern aspects of the country's long seafaring heritage.

Under the direction of its Ruler, HH Sheikh Humaid bin Rashid Al Nuaimi, the local Chamber of Commerce and Industry is now pressing ahead with plans to attract more light-manufacturing firms, which should help further diversify the local economy. The tourist industry, which has grown in recent years, is set to benefit in future from plans for a international airport that will cater primarily for business travel.

The next emirate along the coast, Umm al-Qaiwain, is also developing industry, although more slowly. The main town, of the same name, as with all of the emirates, sits on a peninsula that stretches out into the Arabian Gulf approximately 20 kilometres north of Ajman. With an area of 780 square kilometres, Umm al-Qaiwain has little in the way of resources. This is reflected in its population, which is the smallest of the seven, with an estimated 66,000 inhabitants. However, the development of a small offshore gas and condensate field is expected to provide a substantial boost to the economy.

The desert hinterland of the Emirate, ruled by HH Sheikh Rashid bin Ahmed Al Mu'alla, stretches inland to the oasis of Falaj al-Mu'alla, although for most visitors, the main attractions of the Emirate are its fine beaches, mangrove-fringed lagoons and the important 2,000-year-old archaeological site at Ad Door. Two of the many large-scale residential property now underway in the Emirate capitalize on the charms of its coastline, with further projects inland.

The northernmost part of the UAE's Arabian Gulf coastline is occupied by Ra's al-Khaimah, whose Ruler, HH Sheikh Saqr bin Mohammed Al Qasimi, has been in power since 1948. With an area of 1,700 square kilometres and an estimated population of around 280,000, Ra's al-Khaimah is divided into two parts: one in the Hajar Mountains, near Hatta, and the other the bulk of the fertile Jiri Plain that stretches from Ra's al-Khaimah southwards towards the mineral spa town of Khatt and the village of Idhn.

The birthplace of one of the UAE's greatest historical figures, the 15th century navigator Ahmed bin Majid, Ra's al-Khaimah has long played an important role in the country's history, its ancient port of Julfar having traded as far away as China

With its 100 metre jet of water, Sharjah's Khaled Fountain, in the middle of the lagoon that shares its name, is one of the highest in the world. It presents a spectacular display, especially in the late afternoon.

Abu Dhabi – Garden City of the Gulf

A traditional fishing dhow moored in the small but busy fishing harbour of Ash Sha'am in Ra's al-Khaimah.

for nearly two thousand years. It was also the stronghold of the naval power of the Al Qawasim Sheikhs in the 18th and early 19th centuries.

Although its economy was traditionally based on agriculture and fishing, the Emirate has successfully developed an industrial sector, producing, among other products, ceramic tiles and pharmaceutical products that are exported round the world. A free zone is being developed north of Ra's al-Khaimah town and residential property developments are underway around the old village of Jazirat al-Hamra and its creek. Looking to the future, however, the combination of fertile plains that can be as green as any African savannah after winter rains, and austere, rugged mountains offers considerable potential for the development of the tourist industry.

All but one of the emirates have their capital cities on the Arabian Gulf coast of the UAE. The exception is Fujairah, which lies on the Gulf of Oman coast, and whose population is around 126,000. Its 1,300 square kilometres comprise a mixture of a fertile coastal strip, covered with farms and traditional date-palm groves, and a swathe of the Hajar Mountains. A small part of the Emirate lies on the western side of the mountains, between Habhab and Siji, the latter the home of a flower farm that has succeeded in finding a niche for its blooms in the highly competitive markets of Europe.

Ruled by HH Sheikh Hamad bin Mohammed Al Sharqi, Fujairah has maintained the traditional economic base of agriculture and fishing. It has, at the same time,

The United Arab Emirates

moved steadily and confidently in the development of its shipping industry.

The Port of Fujairah is an important container port, with a large oil-tank farm and small refinery nearby, reflecting the Emirate's position as the second-largest marine-bunkering centre in the world, supplying millions of tonnes of fuel to thousands of passing ships every year. A new 500,000 barrels/day oil refinery is being planned with investment from Abu Dhabi.

The Fujairah Free Zone is the second largest in the country, with an investment worth more than a billion dirhams, while at Qidfa the world's largest reverse-osmosis desalination plant has been built. Supplying power to the whole of the northern emirates, as well as water to Al Ain and Sharjah, it is fuelled by gas imported along a pipeline link through Al Ain.

Fujairah is a favourite weekend destination for residents of other parts of the UAE because of its mountain scenery, historic buildings (including a number of castles and forts), and long beaches, particularly in the northern strip between Dibba and Bidiyah, site of the oldest mosque still to be in use in the country.

The variety of its landscapes has won the Emirate the nickname of 'an Arabian Jewel', and Fujairah is now wisely pinning part of its plans for development on the expansion of its tourist industry. In recent years, several new hotels have been opened, with more being built, particularly along its northern coastline, near Dibba, along with residential developments, to cater for visitors both from home and abroad. These will complement other sectors of an already fast-diversifying economy.

Fujairah's coastal strip, which is ideal for scuba diving, deep-sea fishing and boating, is being geared for tourism.

Abu Dhabi – Garden City of the Gulf

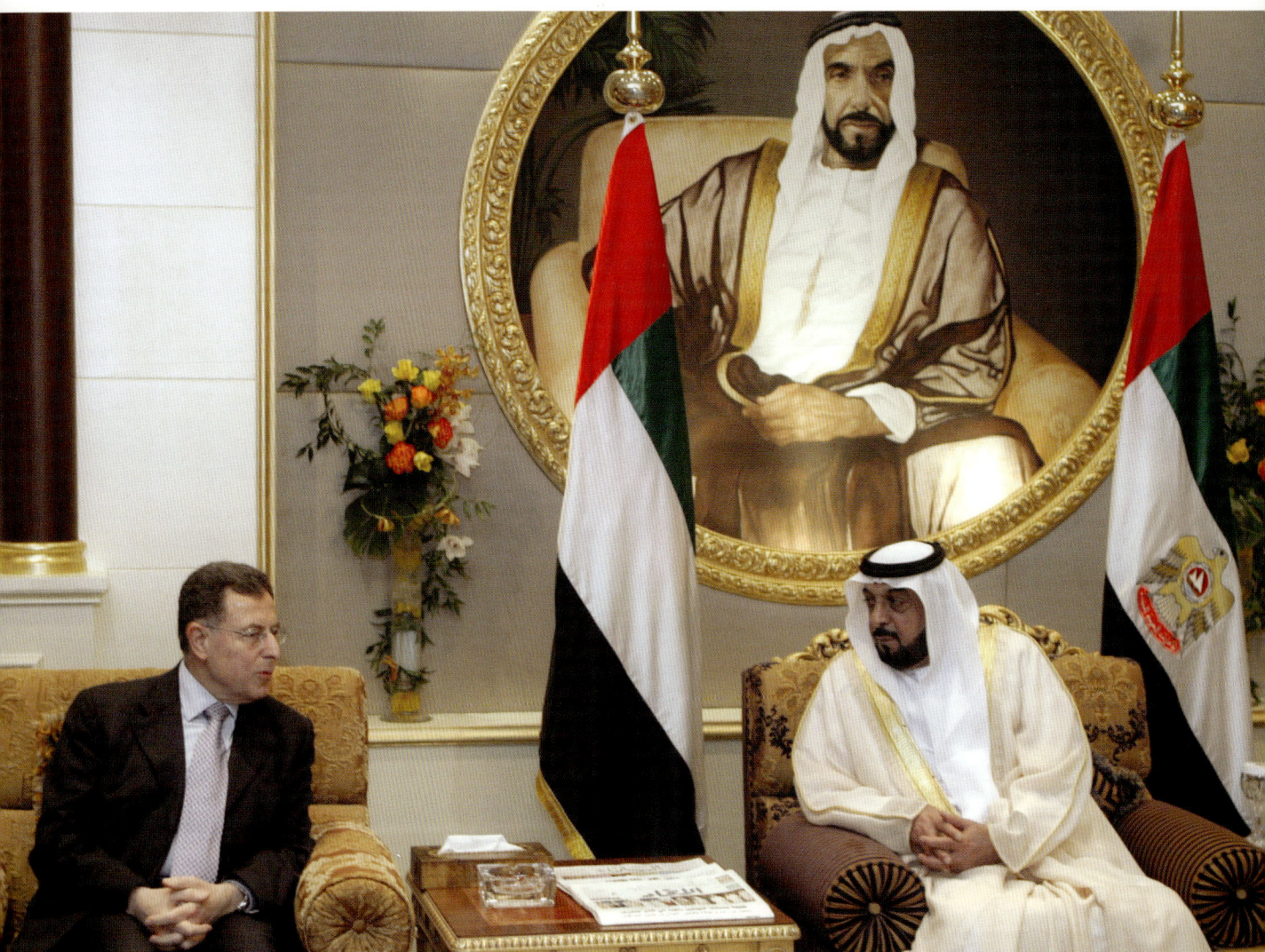

Chapter Two
Ruler and President

Overlooked by a portrait of his father, Sheikh Zayed, Sheikh Khalifa shares Eid greetings with Lebanese Prime Minister, Fouad Siniora.

The Ruler of Abu Dhabi, HH Sheikh Khalifa bin Zayed Al Nahyan, is also the President of the United Arab Emirates, having succeeded his father, the late Sheikh Zayed bin Sultan Al Nahyan, as Ruler on 2 November 2004, and having been elected by his fellow rulers as the UAE's second President on 3 November 2004.

Though still relatively new in the post, Sheikh Khalifa had long been preparing for the tasks he has now assumed, having been appointed as Crown Prince of Abu Dhabi in 1969, and having been closely involved in the government of the Emirate since late 1966.

Born in the inland oasis city of Al Ain in 1948, Sheikh Khalifa was educated locally in one of the first modern schools to be established in the country. On 18 September 1966, following his father's assumption of the post of Ruler of Abu Dhabi a few weeks earlier, he was appointed to succeed Sheikh Zayed as Ruler's Representative in the Eastern Region of Abu Dhabi and was also given the post of Head of the Courts Department in Al Ain. On 1 February 1969, Sheikh Khalifa

Ruler and President

was nominated as the Crown Prince of Abu Dhabi, this being followed on 2 February 1969 by his appointment as the Head of the Abu Dhabi Department of Defence. An early task was that of overseeing the building up of the Abu Dhabi Defence Force, ADDF, which was later to become the nucleus of the United Arab Emirates Armed Forces.

On 1 July 1971, as part of the restructuring of the Government of the Emirate, in advance of the withdrawal by Britain planned for later that year, Sheikh Khalifa was appointed as Prime Minister of Abu Dhabi and its Minister of Defence and Finance. He continued to hold these posts when the federation of the UAE was formally created on 2 December 1971, the date on which the British withdrawal became effective. On the same day, his father, Sheikh Zayed, became the President of the new state and, with the enormous task of building the basis of the federation absorbing much of his father's attention, Sheikh Khalifa was increasingly placed in day-to-day charge of the running of Abu Dhabi.

Sheikh Khalifa succeeded his father as Ruler of Abu Dhabi on November 2, 2004 and was elected President of the United Arab Emirates a day later.

Abu Dhabi – Garden City of the Gulf

Sheikh Khalifa visits the South African arms stand at the biennial International Defence Exhibition (IDEX) that has established Abu Dhabi as the most important centre for defence exhibitions outside Western Europe.

He also took on responsibilities at a country wide level, assuming the post of Deputy Prime Minister in the second UAE Federal Cabinet, formed in December 1973.

Shortly afterwards, when the Abu Dhabi Cabinet was dissolved as part of the process of strengthening the institutions of the UAE federation, Sheikh Khalifa was appointed, on 20 January 1974, as the first Chairman of the Abu Dhabi Executive Council, which replaced the Emirate's Cabinet.

Under his direction, and in accordance with the instructions of Sheikh Zayed, the Executive Council oversaw the implementation of a wide-ranging development programme in Abu Dhabi, including the construction of housing, roads, water and electricity supplies, hospitals and other essential services, and the general infrastructure that led to the emergence of Abu Dhabi as the modern city and emirate of today.

The mid-to-late 1970s were a period of particular growth. The increase in world oil prices that followed the October 1973 Arab-Israeli conflict led to a massive rise in revenues for the Abu Dhabi Government, these being further enhanced by agreements with the foreign oil companies then operating Abu Dhabi's major onshore and offshore oilfields that a majority share in the concessions would be taken by the Government.

A phase of further expansion of oil production then took place, complemented by the beginning of planning for the harnessing of the valuable associated-gas reserves, while, through the Abu Dhabi Investment Authority, of which Sheikh Khalifa became Chairman, surplus funds were deployed into overseas investments.

Within Abu Dhabi, Sheikh Khalifa also paid attention to ensuring that the citizens of the Emirate were able to benefit from growing prosperity, most importantly through the establishment, in 1981, of the Abu Dhabi Department of

Sheikh Khalifa arrives at the Gulf Cooperation Council mid-year summit in Saudi Arabia in 2007. Having been closely involved in the Government of Abu Dhabi since 1966, Sheikh Khalifa is no stranger to these meetings.

Social Services and Commercial Buildings, charged with the provision of loans to citizens for construction. More than Dhs 35 billion was lent by the Department, with more than 6,000 multi-storey buildings being constructed throughout the Emirate before it was restructured in 2005.

The establishment of the Department, popularly known as the 'Khalifa Committee', followed another decision taken by Sheikh Khalifa in 1979 to alleviate the burden on citizens of the repayment of loans from the commercial banks. This involved a fixing of the interest rate payable by citizens of loans for construction at 0.5 per cent, with the balance of the interest being charged by the banks being paid by Government.

As the economy of Abu Dhabi continued to grow during the 1980s, the structure of the oil and gas industry was revised, with the creation of the Supreme Petroleum Council. Chaired by Sheikh Khalifa, this body took over the responsibility for administering the industry, in particular with regard to oil production and pricing policy and the drawing up of a long-term strategy for the sustainable development of Abu Dhabi's enormous oil and gas reserves.

A further step to ensure citizens were able to build the properties they needed, both for residential and for investment purposes, came with the creation by Sheikh Khalifa of the Private Loans Authority, early in 1991, which provides low-interest, long-term loans of up to Dhs 1.2 million.

Sheikh Khalifa has also been extensively involved in other areas of the country's development. In May 1976, following the unification of the armed forces of the Emirates, he was nominated as Deputy Supreme Commander of the UAE Armed Forces. In this capacity, he devoted much attention to building up the country's defensive capability, through the establishment of many military-training

Abu Dhabi – Garden City of the Gulf

Abu Dhabi – Garden City of the Gulf

institutions and through the procurement of the latest military equipment.

At an international level, Sheikh Khalifa has long been associated with the work of the Abu Dhabi Fund for Development, ADFD, which was first established in 1971. Serving for many years as its Chairman, he has supervised its programme of providing financial grants and development aid on concessionary terms to more than 40 countries in Africa, the Arab World and Asia.

Another focus of his attention, and one which has had a measurable impact on the nature of development in Abu Dhabi itself, has been his interest in the conservation of the environment. A keen falconer, like his father, Sheikh Khalifa served for many years as the Chairman of the Environmental Research and Wildlife Debvelopment Agency, ERWDA, now the Environment Agency – Abu Dhabi, EAD, and continues, as President and Ruler, to hold the post of the Agency's Honorary Chairman.

When he took up his dual posts as Ruler of Abu Dhabi and President of the UAE in late 2004, Sheikh Khalifa noted that the key focus of his policy would be to continue to follow the path originally laid down by his father, Sheikh Zayed, seeking to provide the people of the Emirate, both citizens and expatriate residents, with continued social, economic and political security and progress, while, at the same time, making the best use of modern innovations in the practice of government to ensure that Abu Dhabi and the UAE are equipped to meet the challenges of a fast-evolving world.

In this task, he is ably assisted at the Abu Dhabi level by his younger brother, HH Sheikh Mohammed bin Zayed Al Nahyan, formerly Deputy Crown Prince and Chief of Staff of the UAE Armed Forces and now, since November 2004, Sheikh Khalifa's successor as Crown Prince of Abu Dhabi, Chairman of the Abu Dhabi Executive Council and Deputy Supreme Commander of the UAE Armed Forces.

In the short space of time that has ensued since the death of Sheikh Zayed, Sheikh Khalifa and Sheikh Mohammed have launched wide-ranging reforms of the Government of Abu Dhabi, with a major new Government strategy being launched in mid-2007 that outlines plans for the Emirate's development until the year 2030. One focus has been the revamping and streamlining of government departments, with the objective of enhancing both efficiency and accountability. The process of partial privatization that commenced in the electricity and water sector in the late 1990s has now spread to other areas, with a number of services formerly provided by Government, such as waste collection and treatment, being contracted to private companies.

Another focus of attention has been on the need to ensure that the largely desert Western Region of Abu Dhabi, covering some 83 per cent of the Emirate, and more than half of the UAE as a whole, receives more investment, both in terms of services and in terms of job creation.

His key objectives as Ruler and President, Sheikh Khalifa says, will be to continue on the path laid down by his father, Sheikh Zayed, the 'Father of the Nation'.

Born in around 1918 to a younger brother of the Ruler of the day, Sheikh Zayed was named after his illustrious grandfather, Sheikh Zayed bin Khalifa, or 'Zayed the Great', who ruled the Emirate from 1855 to 1909, and raised it to become the dominant power in south-eastern Arabia. During the younger Zayed's childhood and early manhood, the Emirate was far from prosperous, its main source of income, the international trade in pearls, having been brought virtually to a halt as a result of the worldwide recession, the outbreak of the Second World War and the introduction of the Japanese cultured pearl.

The young Zayed spent much of his boyhood in Al Ain, and it was here that he grew to manhood. During the years 1922–1924, when his father Sheikh Sultan was Ruler, he spent more time in the capital, Abu Dhabi, and continued to do so

Top: Qasr al-Hosn was the ancestral home of the Al Nahyan family for nearly two centuries.

Bottom: A 1963 photo of, from right, Sheikh Zayed; his brother the previous Ruler of Abu Dhabi, Sheikh Shakhbut; and a third brother, Sheikh Khaled. A fourth brother, Sheikh Hazza, died in 1958.

when his eldest brother, Sheikh Shakhbut bin Sultan, succeeded an uncle as Ruler in 1928. In his childhood, he took full advantage of the scant opportunities available for education through a traditional Qu'ranic school, and absorbing his knowledge of his family and their people from his relatives.

From roaming in the deserts and mountains, he learned how to survive in the harsh environment, where water was always scarce, and where near-starvation was by no means a stranger. He learned too all he could about the people of the area, the semi-settled farmers of the oases, and the nomadic Bedouin of the desert, with their tales of tribal raids, distant wells and routes across the trackless sands. He watched and listened as tribal elders sought to mediate and conciliate, learning the lesson that in a harsh environment the struggle for mere survival may be the toughest of all.

Drinking deep of the traditions and heritage of his people, he came to develop an unshakeable belief in the religion of Islam, something that remained an essential part of his character throughout his life. He gained the respect and trust of the tribal people, and patriarchs sagely compared the emerging leadership skills of Zayed with those of his grandfather.

As his reputation grew, so did the trust of his brother, Sheikh Shakhbut. When the first geological prospecting team obtained permission to journey through the sands of Abu Dhabi in the 1930s, it was Sheikh Zayed, then still in his teens, who was given the task of guiding them, a first encounter with the world of oil that was later to play such an important part in his life. A few years later, he succeeded in mediating between two desert tribes whose age-old rivalries had broken out into open conflict, winning plaudits for his skills as a conciliator and mediator.

In 1946, a vacancy appeared for the post of the Representative of the Abu Dhabi Ruler in Al Ain. Despite his relative youth, Sheikh Zayed was the obvious choice to undertake the task for his brother. Wise beyond his years and well-versed both in desert lore and in the ways of its people, he was already respected far beyond the borders of Abu Dhabi.

An early European visitor to Al Ain shortly after Sheikh Zayed took up his post was Edward Henderson, then working for Petroleum Development (Trucial Coast) at the beginning of a career in the region spanning nearly five decades. In his memoirs *An Arabian Destiny*, Henderson recalled the impression young Zayed made upon him: "He was then around 30 years old," he wrote. "He was handsome, with humorous and intelligent eyes, of presence and bearing, simply dressed and clearly a man of action and resolution. Although he was young, and had only been formally in charge of the Abu Dhabi section of the oasis and its surrounding deserts for a brief period, he was experienced in the politics of the region, and was already by far the most prominent personality in the area. He had a sure touch with the Bedouin."

In the two decades that followed, refining his knowledge of the practice of governance as he went, Sheikh Zayed was to prove that the confidence shown in him by his brother was by no means misplaced. Under Zayed's leadership, Al Ain embarked on a slow and then explosively fast pace of development.

Recognizing that one of his first tasks was to stimulate the local economy, Sheikh Zayed turned his mind swiftly to the revival of agriculture. Ordering the subterranean channels (the *aflaj*) to be cleaned out, he also ordered the construction of a new one, the Falaj al-Sarouj, the first to be built for many hundreds of years and revised the ancient system of water allocation to permit free access. As a result, it was possible to irrigate formerly neglected land. Agricultural production began to grow, and with it the local economy. Al Ain began, once again, to reassume its traditional position as a market centre for the entire inner desert region.

He also gave orders for the planting of trees along the edges of what were then simple sandy tracks, beginning the process of afforestation and planting that has made Al Ain one of the greenest cities in Arabia today.

As he settled into the task of governing Al Ain, Sheikh Zayed was exposed more and more to the impact of the outside world. By the late 1940s, oil-company officials such as Edward Henderson and the explorer Sir Wilfred Thesiger passed through and stayed with him. The Trucial Oman Scouts, a British-officered force set up at the beginning of the 1950s to keep the peace in the desert, established a camp at Al Ain in one of the traditional forts. From them, Sheikh Zayed learned more about the outside world and the changes taking place.

In 1953, he made his first trip overseas, to Paris and then to London. Amazed by the Eiffel Tower, he was more deeply impressed by the schools and hospitals he visited and decided that his own people should have access to the same facilities.

With Al Ain's place as a regional market re-established, he turned to the need to improve the lot of the people in other ways, using his own funds to establish the first modern school in the Emirate of Abu Dhabi. Among early pupils were his eldest son, Sheikh Khalifa, and other members of the Al Nahyan family.

Meanwhile, events were in train that were to revolutionize the fortunes of Abu Dhabi. After several unsuccessful attempts in the early 1950s, the search for oil eventually paid off, with the discovery first of the Umm Shaif field offshore in 1958, and then the Bab field onshore in 1960. The first cargo of Abu Dhabi's oil

Arabian solidarity: Sheikh Khalifa greets Saudi King Abdullah bin Abdulaziz Al Saud at a GCC summit.

Abu Dhabi – Garden City of the Gulf

In 1960, Murban (Bab)-3 was the first oil well to come on stream in the Emirate of Abu Dhabi.

was exported in 1962. As the rising revenues flowed into the Government's coffers, so too did money become available for development.

On 6 August 1966, acknowledging the necessity for new leadership to meet the challenges facing Abu Dhabi, the Al Nahyan family chose Sheikh Zayed to take over the responsibilities of governing not only Al Ain, but the whole of the Emirate. During the preceding years, Sheikh Zayed had developed a clear vision of how he believed the process of progress should begin. On becoming Ruler, he wasted no time in putting the vision into effect.

Within a matter of weeks, a new structure of government was created and consultants were appointed to advise on roads, schools, hospitals, a port, an airport, and all the other essential parts of the national infrastructure. The process of development had begun, and continues unabated today.

Sheikh Zayed was also faced with the task of creating a new political structure not only for Abu Dhabi but also involving its neighbours. At the beginning of 1968, after a presence in the area that dated back to 1819, the British announced that they would withdraw by the end of 1971. Recognizing that collaboration with the other six emirates of the Trucial States was crucial, Sheikh Zayed agreed with the Ruler of Dubai, Sheikh Rashid bin Saeed Al Maktoum, to establish a federation, and invited the other five rulers to join. By July 1971, agreement was reached, and the new United Arab Emirates (UAE) took its place on the international stage on 2 December, with Sheikh Zayed as President and Sheikh Rashid as Vice-President.

That partnership was to continue until 1990, when Sheikh Rashid died, being succeeded by his eldest son, Sheikh Maktoum, who died in January 2006.

In the more than 30 years that Sheikh Zayed served as UAE President, and the nearly 40 years he was Ruler of Abu Dhabi, the country moved confidently into a new phase of its history, facing the challenges of today and tomorrow with confidence. The pace of the development has been almost breathtaking. The population has grown from 180,000 in 1968 to more than 4.5 million today and schools, hospitals, ports, airports, roads and other facilities cover the country as the revenues from oil and gas production and, increasingly, other industries, are

Ruler and President

Sheikh Zayed always exhibited great love and affection for the children of the Emirates.

directed into stimulating one of the world's fastest-growing economies.

Sheikh Zayed drew great personal satisfaction from what he was able to do for his own people. When one recalls the changes in living standards since he was a boy, that is scarcely surprising. "Thank God that we have been able to achieve all that we sought to achieve for our people," he told one curious interviewer from the *New York Times* in 1998. "At the outset, people questioned whether we would be able to achieve our goals, but, by the grace of God, we have achieved all that we sought, and more, beyond our most ambitious designs."

At one level, the achievement can be viewed in a purely material sense: the building of a modern infrastructure for what is, by any standards, a modern welfare state, where health and education are available for all, and where no one need go to bed hungry. Much of that achievement can be seen elsewhere in this book.

At another level, however, is the fact that the changes that have taken place have come about with the active support and involvement of the people of the Emirates – a society whose traditions date back hundreds of years has absorbed and thrived on change. This can be attributed to the nature of the society itself, and to the wisdom of Sheikh Zayed in ensuring that its time-honoured foundations have been preserved and cherished.

Sheikh Zayed's philosophy of leadership, as with all else in his life, was based upon his deeply held faith in Islam. "It is Islam that asks every Muslim to respect every person," he told another interviewer. "Not, I emphasize, special people, but every person. In short, to treat every person, no matter what his creed or race, as a special soul is a mark of Islam. It is just such a point, embodied in Islam's tenets, that makes us proud of Islam. To be together, to trust each other as human beings, to behave as equals."

That spirit of tolerance is not only fundamental to the nature of UAE society today, but has also been to a very large degree responsible for the way in which the country has been able to develop at such speed, and with such a degree of social harmony over the years. It is a spirit that continues to underpin the philosophy of President His Highness Sheikh Khalifa bin Zayed as he leads Abu Dhabi, and the rest of the United Arab Emirates, confidently into the future.

Abu Dhabi – Garden City of the Gulf

Chapter Three
The Land, its Heritage and People

The Empty Quarter, one of the largest sand deserts in the world, stretches from Abu Dhabi into Oman, Saudi Arabia and Yemen.

Shortly after the conclusion of the Second World War, during 1946–47, Sir Wilfred Thesiger, the last of the great European explorers of the Arabian Peninsula, made his classic journey by camel from southern Oman across the wastes of the Rub al-Khali (the Empty Quarter), to the shores of the Arabian Gulf.

The story, told in his book *Arabian Sands*, is one of intense hardship as he and his Bedouin companions struggled through the trackless, waterless deserts and across the high, rolling dunes, urging their camels onwards to the waterholes and oases and the Gulf beyond. It is an epic story, too, of man's ability to survive in a land where nature itself seems determined to resist his presence.

Part of that journey lay within the Emirate of Abu Dhabi, and Thesiger's descriptions of his arrival in the Liwa Oasis and of his happy interlude hunting in the hinterland of Al Ain with the man who was to become the Ruler of Abu Dhabi and President of the United Arab Emirates, the late Sheikh Zayed bin Sultan Al Nahyan, are not only masterpieces of travel writing, but are also the best available descriptions in the English language of a way of life that has now vanished.

Unlike the other six emirates that together make up the UAE, Abu Dhabi is largely desert, with the dunes imperceptibly but relentlessly moving, year by year, across the land. For countless generations before Thesiger's arrival, the Bedouin of the area had lived and survived – even if they had not thrived – in the harsh

The Land, its Heritage and People

A remote corner of the magnificent Al Jahli Fort in Al Ain, birthplace of Sheikh Zayed in 1918. Sheikh Zayed spent most of his boyhood in Al Ain.

desert conditions. Although today the flow of oil revenues has brought prosperity and development, it is only a recent change.

The 80,000 square kilometres of the Emirate of Abu Dhabi lie on the south-eastern shores of the Arabian Gulf. Bounded by Qatar and Saudi Arabia in the west and south-west; by Oman in the south and east; and by the Emirates of Dubai and Sharjah in the north-east, it is made up mainly of arid gravel plains and sandy deserts, with large areas of *sabkha* (salts flats) along the coast.

Offshore are more than a hundred islands, some large, such as Abu al-Abyadh, others little more than coral outcrops and sandbanks; while in the east, in the Al Ain area, the Emirate's border runs in the lee of the Hajar mountain range, of which the whaleback of Jebel Hafit, south of Al Ain, is an outlier.

The predominant feature is desert, but there are oases in the sands, the best known of which are the large oasis of Al Ain in the east, on the edge of the mountains, and the crescent of small oases known as the Liwa in the south – the last secure source of water before the mountainous dunes of the Rub al-Khali.

Abu Dhabi – Garden City of the Gulf

The Liwa has traditionally been one of the four geographic pillars on which the Emirate of Abu Dhabi stands, the other three being Al Ain, the island of Abu Dhabi and the Western Islands.

Al Ain and the Liwa have traditionally been two of the four geographic pillars on which the Emirate stands, the third being the island of Abu Dhabi, capital both of the Emirate and of the UAE, and the fourth the Western Islands, of which Sir Bani Yas and Dalma are today the most important. All of these have played their part in the history of the Emirate.

The emerging state of Abu Dhabi can be traced back to at least the late-16th century AD. In the latter years of that century, Gasparo Balbi, the court jeweller of the Serene Republic of Venice, toured the Gulf on his way to the East, publishing a book in 1590 in which he names some of the islands. Among them are Daas (Das), Zerecho (Zirku) and Delmephialmas (Dalma), but perhaps the most interesting of the names he reported was Sirbeniast, clearly the island known today as Sir Bani Yas. The reference is the first yet identified to the Bani Yas tribal confederation which, today led by Sheikh Khalifa, is one of the four main tribal groupings making up the indigenous population of Abu Dhabi.

The Bani Yas themselves appear a few decades later, mentioned by name in an old history of Oman as having played a part in a war in the early 17th century that pitted the Omani imams against a tribal alliance which included the Bani Yas and was led by one Nasser bin Qahtan Al Hilali. The Omani history refers to the Bani Yas making use of a fort in the Al Dhafra desert region, west of Abu Dhabi. Coincidentally, work by the Abu Dhabi Islands Archaeological Survey in the Al

Dhafra area, at Mantiqa al-Sirra, has now identified the remains of a long-lost fortress that appears to date from around the same period, although, as yet, no link has been established.

By the late 17th century, the Al Nahyan family appears to have emerged as the undisputed leaders of the Bani Yas confederation, which was based in the Liwa Oasis on the edge of the Rub al-Khali. The Bani Yas shared the Liwa with the Manasir (Mansouris), another of the four tribal groupings that continue to play a major role in the Emirate today, and it was from the Liwa, or so the legend goes, that Sheikh Dhiyab bin Isa sent out a hunting party in 1761 that was to change the history of southern Arabia.

According to tribal tradition, the hunting party followed the track of a gazelle near the coast, and then across a narrow inlet at low tide. When the coastal mist lifted, they saw the gazelle drinking at a spring of brackish water. What happened to the gazelle is not related, but when the party returned to the Liwa to tell Sheikh Dhiyab of their discovery, he decreed that the island should be known as Abu Dhabi (the father or homeland of the gazelle). The truth may, of course, be somewhat more prosaic, for archaeological evidence shows that the island was occupied much earlier, but there is little doubt that the modern settlement dates from around this time.

Recognizing the importance of Abu Dhabi's water, a rare occurrence along the Gulf coastline, Sheikh Dhiyab ordered a village to be established on the island. Although he chose to remain in Liwa, his son and successor, Sheikh Shakhbut bin Dhiyab, moved there in 1795, and Abu Dhabi has been the Emirate's capital ever since. He built a small fort round the spring. Much extended, that fort is today the Al Hosn Palace, or Qasr al-Hosn, long the home of the Government's Centre for Documentation and Research, and soon to be restored as a museum.

After Abu Dhabi and the Liwa, the third pillar of the growing Emirate was Al Ain. This was the traditional home of the powerful Dhawahir (Dhahiri) tribe, with whom Sheikh Shakhbut made an alliance early in the 19th century, building in 1818 a fort whose crumbling remains still survive today. To complete the interlocking tribal alliances that made up the Emirate's population, the Bani Yas also established ties with the nomadic Awamir (Amiri) who roamed over the desert to the south and west of Liwa.

The fourth geographic 'pillar,' the Western Islands, owes its importance to the pearl beds in the surrounding waters which, archaeologists believe, may have been exploited for several thousand years until the trade finally faded away more than half a century ago.

The four tribes and the four geographical pillars, wherein most of the population lived, provided the foundations of the Emirate. The Al Ain oasis, with its lush palm groves and ample supplies of subterranean water flowing through underground channels (or *aflaj*; some as much as 3,000 years old), provided a simple agricultural base, supplemented by the smaller and poorer palms in Liwa and the sparse desert rangeland near by.

The other main source of income was from the waters of the Gulf. The best pearl oyster beds in the Gulf stretch across the great bay extending eastwards from the Qatar Peninsula.

Traditionally, any local boat owner was able to search for pearls on the oyster beds, regardless of his place of origin. Once Sheikh Shakhbut bin Dhiyab had moved his headquarters to Abu Dhabi Island from the Liwa, the oyster beds all fell within Abu Dhabi's waters, giving the growing Emirate additional economic importance. While traders and pearl divers from other areas could continue to operate, they were permitted to do so only if they paid taxes to the Ruler.

Sheikh Shakhbut's own people were also able to profit from the pearling. A pattern of seasonal migration had long existed, to allow the best use to be made of the scanty resources both onshore and offshore. The Bani Yas was a confederation of sub-tribes (all accepting the leadership of the Al Nahyan family), including such names as the Suweidis, the Mazrouis, the Qamzis, the Hamilis, the Qubeisis and the Rumaithis.

Among some groups, the Hamilis and Qubeisis in particular, the winter months were spent in the Liwa or in the desert, while the men went offshore to the pearling grounds during the summer. Other groups, such as the Rumaithis and the Qamzis, could be found primarily along the coast and on the offshore islands, deriving their livelihood from fishing as well as from pearls.

The control of the pearl grounds gave Abu Dhabi the incentive to ensure peace was maintained in the area, as any fighting disrupted the pearl harvest. When, in the period after the arrival of the British in 1820, the imperial power sought to persuade the emirates along the coast to agree to an annual truce at sea during the pearling season, Abu Dhabi accepted with alacrity. The Treaty of Maritime Truce eventually became permanent – giving the area the name by which it was known until independence in 1971, the Trucial States.

From 1855 until 1909, the reign of Sheikh Zayed bin Khalifa (Zayed the Great), a grandson of Sheikh Shakhbut bin Dhiyab, saw Abu Dhabi rise to become a power throughout south-eastern Arabia, with influence stretching deep into inner Oman and the desert wastes of the Rub al-Khali, and up into what now comprises the northern emirates.

Though in subsequent years, the size of the Emirate declined, it retained much of its importance and strategic significance. When the oil wealth began to flow in the early 1960s, Abu Dhabi naturally took a prominent role in the formation of the United Arab Emirates under the father of the present Ruler, Sheikh Zayed bin Sultan, grandson of Zayed the Great.

Relics of an ancient past

If the origins of the present-day Emirate of Abu Dhabi as such date back only 400 years or so, the history of the land and its people go back much further. In recent years, archaeological excavations by both foreign and local teams have shown that it played a prominent role in the development of civilization in this corner of Arabia.

Studies by palaeontologists (fossil specialists) from Britain's Natural History Museum and America's Yale University, as well as teams from the Abu Dhabi Islands Archaeological Survey, and, more recently, from the Abu Dhabi Authority for Culture and Heritage, ADACH, have shown that some six to eight million years ago, during the Late Miocene period, the area west of Abu Dhabi was a land of fertile plains and rivers, where early ancestors of elephants, horses and hippopotami lived.

The rocks in which the fossils have been found, known as the Baynunah Formation, contain the most important array of fossils of land animals from the Late Miocene anywhere in the world. Among major discoveries have been two elephant skulls, two elephant tusks, one more than two metres in length, teeth of hippopotami and horses and crocodile, turtle, fish and bird bones.

It was not until much later, however, that man arrived in the Emirates. The first arrivals seem to have appeared during the Palaeolithic period, perhaps as much as 100,000 years ago. Studies in late 2006 by experts from Britain, working with ADACH, confirmed the presence of Palaeolithic tools near Jebel Dhanna, in the west of Abu Dhabi, with other sites from the same period having been found in Sharjah.

Major settlement appears for the first time during the Late Stone Age, seven and a half thousand years ago. Flint implements in the desert, including

The Land, its Heritage and People

numerous finds in the Umm az-Zamul area, on the edge of the Empty Quarter, can be dated back to around this period, as can flint tool workshops found near Al Ain. Other important evidence has come from the offshore islands, thanks to work by the Government-backed Abu Dhabi Islands Archaeological Survey (ADIAS), now replaced by ADACH.

Under the patronage of His Highness Sheikh Mohammed bin Zayed Al Nahyan, Crown Prince of Abu Dhabi and Deputy Supreme Commander of the UAE's Armed Forces, ADIAS identified two Late Stone Age sites on the island of Marawah, from which more than 200 fine flint tools have been recovered, as well as substantial stone buildings, the earliest pottery ever found in the Emirates, imported from Mesopotamia (modern-day Iraq) around 7,500 years ago, and the skeleton of the UAE's first known inhabitant, dubbed 'Marawah Man' by the archaeologists.

Results from excavations on the island of Dalma in the far west have also been important. Here ADIAS discovered another permanent settlement of approximately the same date, with houses that have floors made of gypsum plaster and which are up to eight metres in diameter, as well as more imported pottery from the early Ubaid civilization in Mesopotamia, showing that the inhabitants of Abu Dhabi's islands were already engaged in maritime trade, precursors of a tradition that has continued until today.

There is further evidence of trading links from several thousand years or so later, from the port-settlement of Umm al-Nar, (now known as Sas al-Nakhl), adjacent to the island-city of Abu Dhabi, where the first archaeological excavations in the Emirates took place more than 40 years ago.

The story of the discovery of the first ancient relics of Abu Dhabi's past would make suitable material for a detective novel. During the 1950s, a Danish team was excavating in Bahrain when the members were informed by a British amateur archaeologist working for Abu Dhabi Marine Areas (ADMA) – an oil company that is now part of the Abu Dhabi National Oil Company group (ADNOC) – that there seemed to be burial mounds on Umm al-Nar.

When the Danes came to look, they found round tombs and a settlement

The main role of the camel today is that of a sporting animal. Races are held throughout the United Arab Emirates in winter, culminating in the great annual races held in April at Al Wathba in Abu Dhabi.

Abu Dhabi – Garden City of the Gulf

The Bronze Age tombs at Hili were excavated by the Danish in the 1960s and have since been the subject of extensive work by the Emirate's own archaeological teams. Many of the historical artefacts from Hili can now be seen in the Al Ain Museum.

dating back to the middle of the third millennium BC, from a culture that was hitherto unknown, and is now named the Umm al-Nar culture.

The site also yielded finds that proved the people of Umm al-Nar were trading copper from the Hajar Mountains, near Al Ain, with Mesopotamia and the Indian subcontinent some 4,500 years ago.

Hearing of the Danish team at work, former UAE President and Abu Dhabi Ruler, Sheikh Zayed, then the Ruler's Representative in Al Ain, came to look at their finds. They should, he told them, visit Al Ain as well, for on the foothills and the crest of nearby Jebel Hafit there were also piles of stones that might be worth examining.

Accepting Sheikh Zayed's invitation, the Danes travelled to Al Ain, to find literally hundreds of tombs on the top of Jebel Hafit, and on the tops of other mountains nearby, dating back, excavation proved, to the early fourth millennium

BC. Those types of grave, now known from throughout the UAE's mountains, have been dubbed 'Hafit tombs'.

Such was the beginning of archaeology in Abu Dhabi and, since then, scarcely a year has passed without an excavation somewhere in the Emirate yielding new information about the area's past. In the early years, apart from Umm al-Nar, much of the work was concentrated in and around Al Ain.

An oasis for at least 5,000 years, its supplies of fresh water were as attractive to early inhabitants as they were in the recent past. Most interesting to the visitor is the complex of sites in the Hili area, which includes a number of settlements, a *falaj* dating back to around 1000 BC, and the now famous Hili Tomb, a round stone structure with bas-relief carvings of men and animals that has been carefully reconstructed. It now stands in the middle of one of Al Ain's lush public gardens, and, like many of the other local sites, is open to visitors.

More recently, the focus has turned to the coast and islands, where a whole range of important discoveries have been made by ADIAS. Among them are the Late Stone Age sites on Dalma and Marawah, previously mentioned; Iron Age fireplaces on Rufayq island; a pre-Islamic Christian monastery on Sir Bani Yas, the first evidence yet found of the presence of Christianity in the UAE before Islam; and the late Islamic fort at Mantiqa al-Sirra in the desert near Medinat Zayed. Further discoveries are made every year, helping to uncover Abu Dhabi's long and fascinating history.

The best of the finds from Umm al-Nar, Jebel Hafit, Hili and other sites in the Al Ain area are on display in the Al Ain Museum, which is housed next to the carefully modernized Eastern Fort. A major new national museum in Abu Dhabi, which will house fossils from the Late Miocene period, as well as archaeological finds, is being planned by ADACH.

The people and their heritage

One popular part of the collection at the Al Ain Museum is an ethnographic display showing how the inhabitants of the Emirate lived in the days before oil – the Bedouin tents, the simple farming implements, the camel saddles and old rifles, all are on display. So too are examples of local jewellery, and other items of everyday use, some of which can still be bought by the discerning buyer from antique shops in both Al Ain and Abu Dhabi.

The display provides the visitor with a brief introduction to the heritage of the people of Abu Dhabi, which, though lacking written literature or imposing non-military architecture, is none the less of considerable interest. Deriving their livelihood both from the land and the sea, the people of Abu Dhabi had a culture before oil that reflected the influences of both – in their sports, in their poetry, in their way of life.

While the oral poetry, naturally, cannot be rendered easily into English, there is poetry enough in the physical aspects of the culture. The great days of the sailing dhows trading with China, India and East Africa, or of the pearling dhows that went out to harvest the Gulf's oysters, have now gone, but the tradition of sailing lives on. Several times a year, there are races for sailing dhows just off the Abu Dhabi Corniche, and the sight of a couple of dozen or more lateen-rigged sails racing against the wind as similar sails have done for centuries certainly has a poetry of its own.

These races are sponsored by the Government, through the Emirates Heritage Club which also supports another local maritime sport seen at the same time as the dhow races, the racing of rowing boats. No coxed fours or eights these – each boat may have up to a hundred oarsmen, chanting ageless rhythmic seamen's songs as they pull their blades through the water.

The preservation of the country's traditional sports is accorded high priority by the Government and, within that context, support has also been given to three land-based sports. The most familiar to the visitor is horse-racing, both with the thoroughbreds of Europe and North America, and with horses of Arab lineage, descended from the ancestors of the great European racing lines. Though unsuited to the deepest deserts, the horse has always been popular in Arabia, and Abu Dhabi has now emerged as a leader in the breeding of traditional Arabian horses. Races are held under the aegis of the UAE Equestrian Federation and the Emirates Arabian Horse Society.

Perhaps the most typical of local sports is falconry, still widely practised today, with saker or peregrine falcons bought from abroad, captured, or, increasingly, bred in captivity, and then trained to answer to their master's voice. From October to March, falcons can be seen on their owners' arms throughout the Emirate, in the car, at home, even in the bank or the shops, but, above all, being trained out on the sands as the Bedouin of Arabia have trained falcons for hundreds of years.

The hunting of the quarry, usually the houbara bustard or the stone curlew, generally takes place abroad, for Abu Dhabi, and the rest of the UAE, now have strict conservation laws to curb local hunting. Through the Environment Agency – Abu Dhabi, EAD, however, a programme for the captive breeding of houbara is now producing a sufficient number of birds for experiments to be undertaken in releasing birds into the wild.

Today, the hunting is carried out from Range Rovers or Toyota Land Cruisers, but until the advent of oil, the falconers rode out on their camels, with hawks on their wrists. Although no longer the preferred mode of transport, the camel remains an integral part of the lives of local people who still keep camels for their milk, and the number of beasts in the Emirate continues to grow year by year, encouraged by Government subsidies for camel owners.

The main role of the camel in Abu Dhabi today, however, is not as a source of milk, or as a means of transport, but as a sporting animal. Every winter, from October to April, camel races are held almost every weekend at tracks throughout the Emirates, culminating with the great annual races in April at Al Wathba, 40 kilometres east of Abu Dhabi, which attract top racers from all round the Arabian Peninsula. With prizes totalling millions of dirhams at stake, it is not surprising that the top camels themselves are worth a considerable sum. Prices of five million or six million dirhams are almost commonplace.

The races themselves provide an opportunity for the visitor to see local society at its most informal and democratic; simple tribesmen from the desert rubbing shoulders with sheikhs in a common fascination with the sport. The expatriate visitor is always welcome – as traditional Arab hospitality demands – but is always an outsider, a guest. These races are a rare feature in Abu Dhabi today, where imported skills, technology and customs prevail in so many aspects of life.

Arab hospitality remains the key to the understanding of the people of Abu Dhabi, and of their country. Forged in the harsh struggle of life before the coming of oil, the hospitality of the Bedouin became a code of conduct. This tradition was so deep-rooted that a traveller coming across a desert encampment could always be sure of food and shelter from what little was available, even if on occasion his hosts were at the same time his tribal enemies.

A philosophy of sharing is, of course, part of the religion of Islam, which took a hold in the Emirates during the lifetime of the Prophet Mohammed (PBUH) and is today a great strength to which the people of Abu Dhabi can hold fast amid the rapid changes that have swept away so much of their previous way of life. It helps to provide, perhaps, a guarantee that however fast and far-reaching the changes, the essential nature of the culture and heritage of the desert people will remain.

Chapter Four
A Thriving Economy

Today, the city of Abu Dhabi, and the Emirate of which it is both capital and main population centre, has a thriving and diversified economy, with a modern infrastructure, social services, a world-class communications and transport system and an industrial base that ranges from oil and gas, petrochemicals and heavy industry to light manufacturing, agriculture and the services and tourism sectors.

Coupled with the possession of extensive international investment and reserves, it is well equipped to grow steadily in the years ahead.

Indeed, the Emirate is now on the threshold of a major economic transformation designed to be built in partnership with a private sector that is open, diversified, innovative, export-oriented, capital and knowledge intensive, and yet, at the same time, is still dependent to a considerable extent on revenues from the oil and gas industry to fuel its growth. During the period 2006–2010, Abu Dhabi is expected to invest more than Dhs 367 billion in numerous large-scale projects, ranging from an expansion of the oil and gas industry, including the development of new fields, to heavy industry such as aluminium, residential and commercial property development and literally dozens of new hotels to cater for the rapidly-growing tourist industry.

Yet, little more than 40 years ago, the city of Abu Dhabi itself was not much more than a poor coastal village while, inland, the way of life had hardly changed for centuries.

The Emirate's local stock exchange, the Abu Dhabi Securities Market, was formally established in 1999 to regularize trading in securities and offers opportunities for trading in a number of listed local stocks.

Abu Dhabi – Garden City of the Gulf

The modern, glass-clad tower blocks of Abu Dhabi are the second generation of modern buildings on the island.

Traditionally, the people of Abu Dhabi survived in a subsistence economy. Fishing and, in the inland oases, agriculture, provided the essentials of life for the settled people, while the nomadic tribes depended primarily on the herding of their livestock. In the mountains near Al Ain, reserves of copper ore had been exploited from around 3000 BC, but this early industry died out in the medieval period. Another industry, that of mining sulphur at Jebel Dhanna, in the west, enjoyed a short-lived boom for a couple of centuries or so in the 17th and 18th centuries, but also came to an end.

Offshore, another important industry, that of harvesting the fine pearls found on the Gulf's oyster beds, had commenced even earlier than the copper trade, more than 7,000 years ago, and had thrived well into the 20th century. The introduction in Japan of the cultured pearl, followed by the worldwide depression of the 1930s and the Second World War, however, dealt successive blows to the pearling industry and, by the early 1950s it had virtually disappeared.

Just in time, another resource was discovered – that of oil. Exploration began after the Second World War and, following more than a decade of searching, the first commercially viable reserves were identified in the late 1950s. In 1962, Abu

Dhabi became an oil exporter for the first time (*see next chapter*).

Throughout the years that have followed, Abu Dhabi's economy has been underpinned by the oil industry, which has grown despite the vicissitudes of the international oil market. Revenues from oil and, later, natural gas, as well as from overseas investments made with the surplus oil revenue, have flowed into the coffers of the Government in such amounts that it has been possible for huge projects to be funded consecutively.

In the early years of Abu Dhabi's development, the growth sectors of the economy were based almost entirely on the oil industry and on government expenditure and employment that, apart from a small, but rapidly growing civil service, was also heavily linked to the oil sector.

At the same time, the Government, headed by the late President and Ruler, Sheikh Zayed bin Sultan Al Nahyan, recognized that oil and gas were resources that were being depleted and that it was unwise to permit a situation where the health of the economy was dependent upon one single source to continue.

Through the Abu Dhabi Executive Council, chaired by HH Sheikh Khalifa bin Zayed, Crown Prince of Abu Dhabi from 1969 until he became Ruler in 2004, and now by his successor as Crown Prince, HH Sheikh Mohammed bin Zayed, steps have been taken to lessen this dependence. Although revenues from oil and gas and overseas investments continue to be a mainstay of the local economy, a growing industrial sector is now being paralleled by rapid growth in tourism and property development as well as a range of other services.

A Policy of Diversification

The policy of diversification began with initiatives to promote downstream investment, such as petrochemical plants, in the oil-and-gas sector and light industry. In recent years, this has broadened, with Government investment now going into a much wider range of industries, such as shipbuilding, steel-manufacturing plants and two aluminium smelters. The increasing sophistication of Abu Dhabi's private sector has also meant that local businessmen have also become deeply involved, often in partnership with Government or with overseas investors, bringing a new spirit of entrepreneurial innovation.

In 1968, when the first census was carried out, the Emirate of Abu Dhabi had an estimated population of only 46,500. By mid-2007, it was estimated to be approaching two million, the majority of whom lived in the capital and its satellite townships on the mainland and most of the others in and around Al Ain – although townships such as Mirfa, Bida (Medinat) Zayed and Ruwais, in the Western Region, are also growing rapidly.

The rate of unemployment is enviably low and the labour force is growing rapidly as a result of the many new projects being implemented, although there is a widely recognized need for more opportunities to be made available for the UAE's own citizens in all sectors of the economy.

More than 90 per cent of the Emirate's workforce is expatriate, largely from the Indian subcontinent, with large communities also from Iran, and elsewhere in Asia, such as China and the Philippines. There are also significant communities from other Arab states, including Egypt, Palestine, Lebanon and Syria, and from Europe and North America, in particular from Britain, France, the United States and Canada.

Employment and Emiratization

With a rapidly rising number of UAE citizens or nationals, the Government is actively promoting a programme of 'Emiratization', which is leading to a growing number of nationals, both men and women, entering the workforce. Besides

Government ministries and departments, this process is particularly visible in the oil and gas sector and in the finance, services and tourism industries, while many young UAE citizens are now choosing to set up their own businesses to take advantage of the new opportunities being provided.

Key sectors of employment are currently the civil service, including both federal ministries and departments of the local government; the services sector, including banking, finance and the hotel-and-tourism industry; the industrial sector, covering both the oil and gas industry; and, increasingly, other areas of heavy industry; light industries; transport and communications; and agriculture.

The Financial Sector

Abu Dhabi has developed an extensive and sophisticated financial sector, that serves local customers and interacts with global markets. The UAE Central Bank, which is based in Abu Dhabi, supervises the local institutions and also regulates the activities of all foreign banks in the Emirates, as well as currency-exchange houses and financial advisers. Formed in 1981, the Central Bank has been an effective force for stability and has enabled the economy to weather a number of crises. Its functions have grown as the financial sector has developed.

In recent years, as the stock markets in Abu Dhabi and Dubai have been formed and have grown, the UAE Central Bank has taken on the responsibility of regulation in this area while it also provides guidance to local banks and to the local branches of foreign banks on the amount of leverage they are permitted to offer to UAE investors applying for share allocations in the numerous Initial Public Offerings (IPOs) on offer as new companies in property, oil and gas, and other sectors, tap the local market for funds.

A third new area of activity, of major importance following the September 2001 terrorist attacks on the United States, has been increased regulation and monitoring of money transfers, as part of the international efforts to eradicate money laundering.

The first commercial bank in Abu Dhabi opened as recently as in 1959, a branch of the British Bank of the Middle East, now HSBC. There are six Abu Dhabi-based local banks, of which the National Bank of Abu Dhabi (NBAD) is the largest. Indeed, it was for many years the largest bank in the UAE, although a

Typical of many of the striking buildings in Abu Dhabi, Marina Mall combines modern design concepts with strong Arabian themes.

merger of two Dubai-based banks in 2007 reduced it to a second-place ranking. During 2006, it recorded a net profit of Dhs 2.105 billion, with total assets having risen from around Dhs 31 billion in 1999 to Dhs 100.9 billion at the end of 2006.

The second largest, Abu Dhabi Commercial Bank, saw its assets rise from Dhs 57.7 billion at the end of 2005 to Dhs 81.1 billion at the end of 2006, a rise of 41 per cent, while its net profit during the same period rose by 12 per cent to Dhs 2.147 billion. The most rapidly growing local bank, First Gulf Bank, saw its net assets more than double, to Dhs 26 billion, in 2005, and then rise again sharply to Dhs 47.76 billion in 2006, with net profit rising in 2006 to Dhs 1.535 billion, with further dramatic growth in the first half of 2007. Union National Bank, whose total assets at the end of 2006 were around Dhs 41.5 billion, up by nearly 19 per cent over the previous year, recorded net profits for the year of Dhs 1.007 billion.

The other two banks are both Islamic institutions. The Abu Dhabi Islamic Bank, once the largest Islamic financial institution in the world, with paid-up capital of Dhs 1 billion, commenced full operations in early 1999. Operating in accordance with Sharia law, it had total assets of Dhs 36.3 billion at the end of 2006, up from Dhs 22.2 billion at the end of the previous year, while net profits during the same period rose from Dhs 345 million to Dhs 571 million.

In early 2007, plans were announced by the Abu Dhabi Government for the establishment of Al Hilal (Crescent) Bank, which will have a paid up capital of Dhs 4 billion. Wholly owned by the Government, Al Hilal is expected to play a major role in the development of Islamic banking and finance within the region.

Banks from the other emirates also have branches in Abu Dhabi, as do many major global banks, all competing for a share of the lucrative market for institutional business, trade finance and personal banking.

Besides the banking sector, Abu Dhabi has a number of other financial institutions. Of particular importance are the currency-exchange houses, some of which are little more than money changers in the souk, others major financial institutions in their own right, handling hundreds of millions of dollars a year in currency exchange, transfers and drafts. Their services are particularly valued by Abu Dhabi's expatriate labour force, many of whom come from rural areas in countries such as India, Pakistan and the Philippines, where the indigenous banking system is poorly developed.

The local stock exchange, the Abu Dhabi Securities Market, was formally established in 1999 to regularize trading in securities and offers opportunities for trading in a number of listed local stocks, including key firms such as the locally incorporated banks, telecommunications giant Etisalat, industrial enterprises such as Abu Dhabi Shipbuilding and others.

In recent years, a number of new companies have come to the market, one example being Aabar Petroleum Investment Company, the first local firm engaged in the oil and gas industry to offer shares to the public, which has extended its interests well beyond the UAE, taking over a Singapore-based oil company with interests in Indonesia, Philippines, Thailand and Vietnam in early 2006. The market is linked with another trading floor in Dubai and together the two have opened up greater opportunities for UAE citizens and companies to invest in local firms.

The door is now being gradually opened to foreign investors, who can buy shares in many of the listed companies, part of the way in which the UAE is becoming increasingly intertwined with the global economy.

A much less visible part of the financial community is the Abu Dhabi Investment Authority (ADIA), which is overseen by the Abu Dhabi Investment Council (ADIC), established in 2006, both of which are chaired by Sheikh Khalifa. Established before the creation of the UAE to act as fund manager for Abu Dhabi's surplus oil revenues, ADIA is now one of the world's major investment

Abu Dhabi – Garden City of the Gulf

institutions and, although it never gives any indication of the total funds under its management, a cautious estimate would certainly suggest that these are in excess of Dhs 2,200 billion.

Now, in association with another government-controlled body, the Mubadala Development Company (MDC), ADIA is working to implement a strategy to attract more foreign investment to Abu Dhabi. Mubadala, which holds the Government stake in a number of major enterprises, has also, like ADIA, extended its interests overseas with the objective of creating blue-chip partnerships that will be, both directly and indirectly, of benefit the local economy. One such partnership, made in 2005, involved taking a strategic stake in car manufacturer Ferrari, building an alliance with its controlling shareholder Fiat that has already brought returns with a plan for a joint project in Abu Dhabi.

A Vibrant Commercial Sector

Abu Dhabi's vibrant commercial sector is now being driven by a combination of Government and private-sector initiatives, a result of a partnership that's become increasingly active since the governmental reforms introduced after the accession of Sheikh Khalifa in late 2004. A large part of the process has been stimulated by the decision to reduce the direct responsibility of Government for services in a wide variety of sectors.

Following a period of 35 years, during which Government initiatives drove the country's development, the time is now right for privatization of services and

Abu Dhabi's Mubadala Development Company has a number of key partnerships with overseas companies, including prestigious car manufacturer Ferrari whose formula one racing cars should be seen competing in the Abu Dhabi Grand Prix scheduled to be held on Yas Island from 2009.

A Thriving Economy

industries that are not the core business of government, and this process is expected to develop rapidly as part of the planning laid down for development of the Emirate from now until 2030.

The process of privatization first got under way with the complete reorganization of Abu Dhabi's water and electricity sector in the late 1990s. Power and water is now supervised by the Abu Dhabi Water and Electricity Authority, ADWEA, under which six separate power-generation and desalination companies have been established to run the power plants.

The biggest of these is the Taweela complex, north-east of Abu Dhabi, in an area that's being developed as a major industrial centre. The Dolphin Energy gas pipeline from Qatar (see 'Oil and Gas'), also makes its landfall here, while projects currently getting under way include an aluminium smelter, being built as a joint venture between the Dubai Aluminium Company (DUBAL), owned by the Government of Dubai, and Mubadala, and another smelter, being built in partnership with international mining giant Rio Tinto, which will be located near Ruwais, in the Western Region. When completed, these will be the largest of their type in the world. Taweela will also be the location for Abu Dhabi's new port, Port Khalifa, and an associated industrial zone.

Other major developments in the power and water sector have included the construction of large plants in Abu Dhabi's Western Region, one between Jebel Dhanna and the island of Shuweihat and another at Mirfa, to complement the existing, but smaller, plants on Abu Dhabi island, near Mina Zayed, and on the

nearby island of Umm al-Nar (recently renamed Sas al-Nakhl). The major plants are all now being run as joint ventures between ADWEA and foreign utility firms, who then sell the water and electricity they produce to two locally owned distribution companies. During the next few years, the sector is expected to expand rapidly in order to meet rising demand from domestic, commercial and industrial users.

The part-privatization of the water and electricity sector has been a major success and local investors are now able to buy shares in some of the companies, alongside major industrial firms from overseas. It has since been followed by a further relinquishment by Government of its responsibility for other utilities and services, initiated by a total re-structuring of the Government of the Emirate that took place at the end of 2004. This was followed, in mid-2007, by the announcement of the long-term strategy for the Emirate's development that will continue until 2030.

Among these have been the transferring of the responsibility for refuse collection from the local municipalities in Abu Dhabi and Al Ain, now part of a newly created Department of Municipalities and Agriculture, to a privately owned company and a trimming back of the agricultural programme.

More dramatic, both in terms of visibility and in terms of the direct impact on the economy, has been the opening up of the economy to stimulate much-needed private investment in the developing of residential property and hotels. Following the passing of legislation to allocate areas for private property development, several companies have been established that have announced a slew of new mixed-use projects.

Among the first to get going have been Aldar Properties, an offshoot of Mubadala, and the Tourist Development Investment Company (TDIC), an offshoot of the Abu Dhabi Tourism Authority (ADTA), along with a number of others, such as Surouh Real Estate, Reem Investments and Al Qudra.

Aldar alone has announced plans for the construction of more than 30 new hotels by the end of 2010, as well as large residential developments at Al Raha Beach, just off Abu Dhabi island; at Al Qurm, on the western side of Abu Dhabi island; and a mixed-use residential and commercial development of the Central Market area of downtown Abu Dhabi. The flagship project for TDIC is a massive, mixed-use development project on Saadiyat Island, just north-east of Abu Dhabi city, which will also include a world-class Cultural District, with branches of France's Louvre Museum and the US-based Guggenheim Museum. Overall, by 2015, at least 100 new hotels will have been built.

The drive for new construction is involving both the re-development of already built-up areas and the development of new 'greenfield' sites. On Abu Dhabi island, for example, the site of the old Abu Dhabi Tourist Club, a popular leisure spot since the 1970s, is being re-developed as a luxury residential community, with villas, commercial and residential buildings and a marina, while much of the area of Port (Mina) Zayed will also be turned over for development once shipping activity is moved to the new Khalifa Port at Taweela.

Islands adjacent to Abu Dhabi, such as Saadiyat, Reem and the man-made Lulu Island, just off the city's Corniche, are also being developed, as well as areas on the mainland, including Al Raha Beach and Al Bahia, a little to the north-east.

Expanding Industry

While the oil and gas industry continues to provide the focus of Abu Dhabi's industrial sector, a fresh impetus has been given in recent years by initiatives designed to promote other industries.

Perhaps the most important of these is the Higher Corporation for Specialized

A Thriving Economy

Economic Zones (HCSEZ), or ZonesCorp, created in 2004, which has launched plans for industrial cities. One is at Ruwais, in the west, and is primarily related to oil and gas. The second, the Industrial City of Abu Dhabi Two, ICAD-2, situated at Musaffah on the mainland just south-west of Abu Dhabi island, is designed as a mixed industrial zone that will accommodate companies dealing with the construction industry, the oilfield services industry, car manufacturing and assembly, food and textiles, plastic and chemicals, high-tech industries and others. During the next few years, it is expected to grow to cover more than 50 square kilometres and one particular attraction for overseas investors in ICAD-2 is a law passed in 2005 to permit 100-per-cent foreign ownership of projects.

A Dhs 2 billion steel-manufacturing plant is one of the new projects that have already been agreed, while the Abu Dhabi Shipbuilding Company, part government-owned and partly owned by private shareholders, which grew out of the Government's military Offsets Programme, is another major employer – offering the largest facilities of its kind anywhere in the Arabian Gulf.

The objective of the HCSEZ is to establish high-value industry clusters that will help to transform the Emirate into an industrial, services and logistics hub for the region.

Alongside the development of industry and tourism, the Emirate is continuing to build on its already successful conference and exhibitions business. The most important event is the biennial International Defence Exhibition (IDEX) which, since it was first held in 1993, has established Abu Dhabi as the most important centre for defence exhibitions outside Western Europe, attracting both the world's major defence manufacturers as exhibitors and senior government and

A visual sign of Abu Dhabi's wealth is the seemingly endless construction of remarkable buildings, fashioned from modern materials to reflect and complement the more traditional Islamic styles surrounding them. This is epitomized by the seven-star Emirates Palace hotel located at the start of the Breakwater.

military personnel from round the world. The new facilities at the Abu Dhabi National Exhibitions Company, ADNEC, site, near Zayed Sports City, are being complemented by new hotels and mixed-use residential and commercial development that, when completed, will provide Abu Dhabi with the finest exhibition complex in the Gulf.

Modern Infrastructure

Since the UAE federation was founded in 1971, substantial investment has been put into providing the very best in modern communications. Within the country itself, a fine road network connects the capital with Dubai and the other northern emirates, as well as Al Ain and with the oil industry town of Ruwais inland in the west, the highway to the latter continuing on through the Ghuweifat border post and away to the rest of the Middle East. Other roads run deep into the desert and on to the agricultural centre of the Liwa Oasis on the edge of the Empty Quarter. In all, the Emirate has more than 1,500 kilometres of highways, excluding internal roads in the major population centres. A railway link, both to Dubai and the northern emirates and away to the west and the rest of the Arabian Peninsula is also being planned.

Also facilitating internal, and external, communications is the state-of-the-art telecommunications network provided by state-owned Etisalat that, by mid-2007, had nearly six million subscribers to its mobile services, 1.3 million subscribers to the fixed-line network and more than 2.5 million internet users. A recent entrant into the telecommunication fields, du, which began operations in early 2007, had a further half million mobile customers, making the UAE, as a whole, the country with the highest penetration rate for telecoms in the entire region. Etisalat, through the locally based regional satellite firm Thuraya, is also emerging as the Middle East's leader in the telecommunications industry.

Connections with the rest of the world are provided through excellent air and sea links and, here again, the Government has been actively divesting itself of direct control over the infrastructure. In early 2006, the former Department of Civil Aviation was wound up and was replaced by the Abu Dhabi Airports Company (ADAC), which is now responsible for the Emirate's two international airports, at Abu Dhabi and Al Ain. 100 per cent owned by Government, ADAC may later bring in strategic partners to diversify ownership.

Abu Dhabi International Airport, 40 kilometres outside the city, is currently in the throes of a major expansion programme launched in 2005, with the construction of a temporary second terminal that will nearly double handling capacity to 6.8 million passengers a year. In the same year, a massive re-development programme, that will see a new runway, capable of taking the latest wide-bodied passenger jets, such as the Airbus A380, and a new control tower and other facilities, commenced. Overall, the programme is expected to cost some Dhs 25 billion. By 2010, when the first phase is scheduled for completion, the airport will be able to handle 20 million passengers a year, tripling the 2006 capacity. Additional cargo facilities and a large free zone are also being constructed.

All of these will prove of enormous value to Abu Dhabi-owned Etihad Airlines, the UAE's national carrier. Commencing operations in November 2003, the airline won the 'World's Leading New Airline Award' at the World Travel Awards in December 2004, and has continued to win the award in successive years. By mid-2007, it was already flying to more than 40 destinations, including North America, and plans to fly to 70 destinations by 2010, with both passenger and cargo services, by which time its fleet should have grown to more than 60 aircraft.

Besides having an award-winning duty-free complex, Abu Dhabi Airport is also home to the region's only major aviation maintenance centre, run by Abu Dhabi

Aircraft Technologies, established in late 2007 to replace the former Gulf Aircraft Maintenance Company (GAMCO). By 2012, ADAT plans to invest more than Dhs 1,800 million in expanding facilities and entering new markets through partnerships, joint ventures and potential acquisitions, making Abu Dhabi a regional centre for the aviation industry. The airport is also the base of Abu Dhabi Aviation, the largest commercial helicopter operator in the Middle East.

Abu Dhabi's second commercial airport, at Al Ain, 100 kilometres to the east of the capital, is also being expanded, and is expected to become of increasing importance in terms of incoming tourist traffic.

While the oil and gas industry operates its own ports and terminals, the bulk of Abu Dhabi's shipping-industry needs has traditionally been focused on Mina (Port) Zayed, on the north-eastern tip of Abu Dhabi island, which opened in the early 1970s and which, by 2006, was handling nearly four million tonnes of cargo a year.

Now, though, a major new port, Khalifa Port, with an adjacent industrial zone, is to be developed adjacent to the power-and-water-desalination complex at Taweela, some 40 kilometres north-east of Abu Dhabi. The management of Port Zayed, which is expected to cease operations by around 2010, and the new Khalifa Port, as well as other, smaller, ports, is being undertaken by the newly established Abu Dhabi Ports Company (ADPC), through a subsidiary, Abu Dhabi Terminals Company. ADPC has replaced the old Abu Dhabi Seaports Authority, another result of the restructuring of government to bring in a more business-orientated approach.

Khalifa Port will be operated by Dubai Ports World, which has become one of the world's leading players, bringing synergy to the operations of the UAE's major ports. Investment in the first phase will be some eight billion dirhams, with an even larger investment expected during the second phase.

The X-shaped Midfield Terminal Complex, the striking centrepiece of the new-look Abu Dhabi International Airport. An investment of US$6.8 billion should see the airport's passenger capacity increase from seven million to 21 million by 2010.

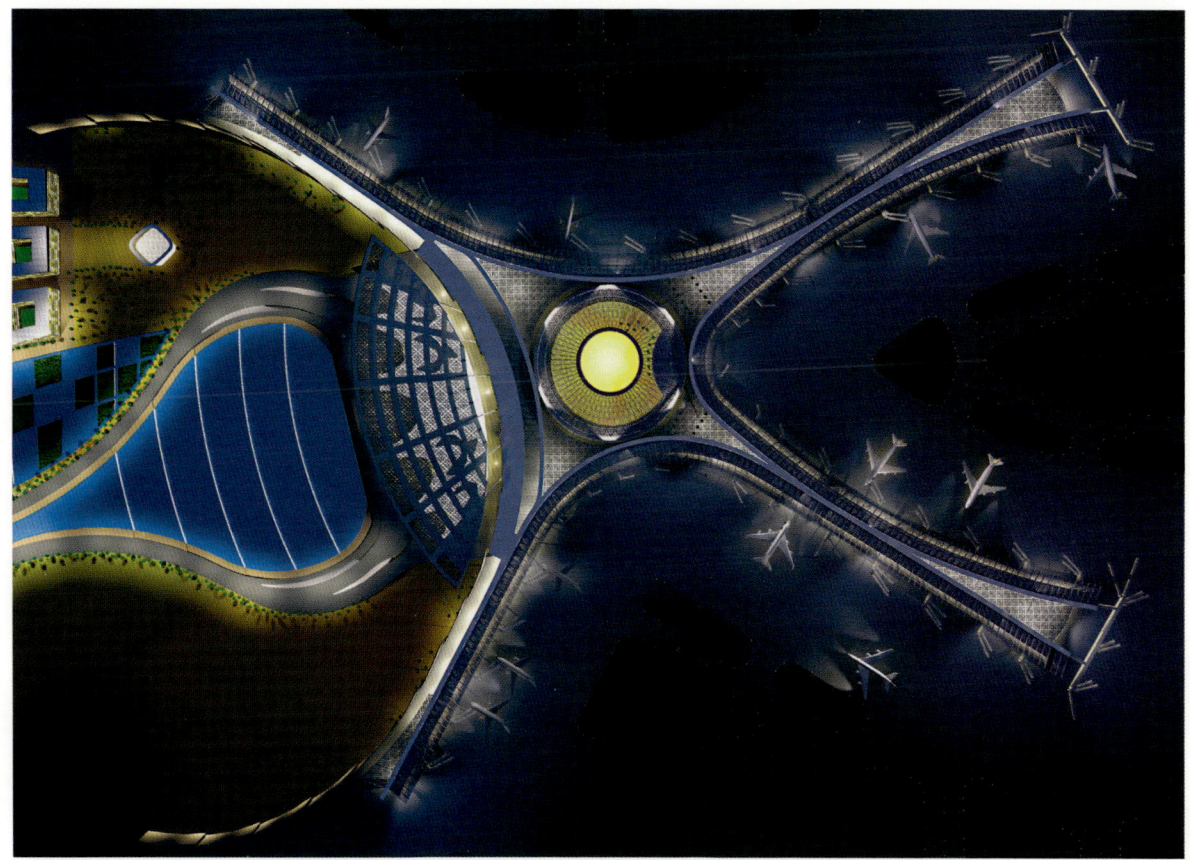

Abu Dhabi – Garden City of the Gulf

Chapter Five
The Oil and Gas Sector

The spudding-in ceremony at Ra's Sadr in 1950. At nearly 4,000 metres it was, at the time, the deepest ever drilled in the Middle East but was a dry hole.

The Emirate of Abu Dhabi, and the seven-member federation of the United Arab Emirates (UAE) of which it is a part, is one of the fastest growing states in the world. Half a century ago, life in the Emirates was little changed from what it had been hundreds of years earlier. As recently as the early 1970s, just after the UAE itself was formed, cities such as Abu Dhabi, today a thriving modern metropolis, were still small towns.

The pace of growth has been dramatic. While much of the credit belongs to the country's rulers, led from 1971 to 2004 by former President Sheikh Zayed bin Sultan Al Nahyan and now by his son and successor, President His Highness Sheikh Khalifa bin Zayed, little could have been achieved without the revenues from oil and gas production, which have underpinned the economy and have provided the fuel for growth.

In the words of Sheikh Zayed: "Oil is useless if it is not exploited for the welfare of the citizen," and, in the years since 1966 when he became Ruler of Abu Dhabi, the country's oil wealth has indeed been used to provide the people of the Emirates with all the facilities of a modern welfare state and to make it possible for a widespread programme of diversifying the economy so that the country as a whole is no longer solely dependent on its depleting energy reserves.

Today, the UAE is one of the world's top oil producers, with its proven

The Oil and Gas Sector

Much of Abu Dhabi's oil wealth comes from offshore fields, where giant platforms such as this TotalFinaElf structure are operated with foreign partners.

recoverable reserves of around 98 billion barrels being the fifth largest in the world and nearly 10 per cent of the world's total. With six trillion cubic metres of gas reserves as well (also the fifth largest in the world), the country is well equipped to continue production of both oil and gas in substantial quantities for more than a century. In excess of 90 per cent of those oil reserves are in the Emirate of Abu Dhabi, whose people are among the richest on earth, in terms of per capita income.

The first commercially viable oil discovery in the Emirates, and in Abu Dhabi, was not made until 1958, and production did not begin until 1962. The history of the Emirate's oil industry, however, can be traced back nearly 70 years.

Oil production commenced in Iraq and Iran prior to the First World War, but little attention was then paid to the southern Gulf. In the early 1930s, however, the discovery of oil further north in the Arabian Peninsula – in Bahrain and Saudi

Abu Dhabi – Garden City of the Gulf

Arabia – sparked the interest of the major western oil companies in the little-known emirates of the lower Gulf, the largest of which was Abu Dhabi. Front-runner in the field was the consortium of foreign oil companies forming the Iraq Petroleum Company (IPC). This included British Petroleum (BP), Shell and the companies now known as Total and ExxonMobil, as well as the family interests of famed Armenian entrepreneur Calouste Gulbenkian, the original 'Mr Five Per Cent'. In the mid-1930s, IPC obtained permission to venture into the Emirates.

The first step was to send teams of surveyors to see whether there were any surface indications of oil or any interesting geological structures. Visiting the offshore islands was easy: the first known landing of a motor vehicle on Abu Dhabi's western island of Sir Bani Yas dates back to this time, when an oil company survey party put a truck onshore to help them move around. Venturing inland, however, was much more difficult. At the time, little was known about the desert areas of Abu Dhabi except by the local inhabitants. Indeed it was not until the late 1940s that the first European explorer, Sir Wilfred Thesiger, set sight on the Liwa Oasis after one of his epic crossings of the Empty Quarter. There was also no guarantee that the Bedouins of the desert would welcome the visitors.

The ruler of Abu Dhabi, Sheikh Shakhbut bin Sultan Al Nahyan, elder brother and predecessor of the late Sheikh Zayed, welcomed the wish of the oil companies to start exploring, although one of his main concerns was that they should also help to find new supplies of fresh water for the people. To show his own backing for their enterprise, he assigned the young Sheikh Zayed to accompany them.

Initial signs were promising and, in January 1939, after several years of negotiations, Sheikh Shakhbut signed an exploration concession with an IPC subsidiary, Petroleum Concessions Limited (PCL), which covered the whole of the territory of Abu Dhabi for a period of 75 years. PCL established its own subsidiary, Petroleum Concessions (Trucial Coast), to operate this concession and others it won in the rest of the Emirates. Later renamed Petroleum Development (Trucial Coast) and then finally the Abu Dhabi Petroleum Company (ADPC), it continued

Adma-Opco has a super-complex at Umm Shaif in Abu Dhabi waters. Abu Dhabi's oil era began when oil was struck in commercial quantities at Umm Shaif-1 in 1962.

to operate onshore until 1979, when it handed over the task to a new company, the Abu Dhabi Company for Onshore Oil Operations, ADCO, 60 per cent owned by the Abu Dhabi National Oil Company, ADNOC, with the ADPC shareholders holding the remaining 40 per cent.

Plans to examine the new concession area were delayed by the onset of the Second World War, and it was not until later in the 1940s that exploration began in earnest. Using sturdy vehicles and engaging Bedouin as guides, the geologists spread out across the land to choose the site for their first well.

Onshore Fields

The site chosen was at Ra's Sadr, on the coast some 35 kilometres north-east of Abu Dhabi, where the spudding of the UAE's first oil well took place in 1950. The operation was not without incident and drama. All of the equipment had to be brought in by barge to Ra's Ghanadha, a few kilometres further east, then brought overland to the drilling site. At one point, dissatisfied with their conditions of employment, the locally hired Abu Dhabian work-force downed tools, and, in the last recorded use of British 'gunboat diplomacy' in the Gulf, a force of Royal Marines was landed to bring the dispute to an end.

Former IPC official Ronald Codrai recalled years later that there was an element of farce to the affair. The boats used by the Royal Marines grounded in the shallow waters and they were obliged to seek help from local fishermen to get to Ra's Sadr. Fortunately, wiser counsels prevailed, and another brother of Sheikh Shakhbut, Sheikh Hazza, persuaded the oil company to improve its terms and encouraged its employees to go back to work.

At the time it was drilled, the Ra's Sadr-1 well, more than 3,960 metres (13,001 feet) in depth, was the deepest ever drilled in the Middle East – early proof of the fact that the local oil industry was to be at the forefront of petroleum technology. Nevertheless, it was a dry hole, as was a second well drilled at Shuweihat, near Jebel Dhanna. A third at Murban, west of Abu Dhabi and in

Exploration for new oil wells and the regular development of existing wells in Abu Dhabi ensures maximum production capacity is achieved and maintained.

Abu Dhabi – Garden City of the Gulf

Jack-up rigs stacked in Abu Dhabi's Mina Zayed. A number of new oil finds have been proven in the emirate and are being kept in reserve for future production.

the heart of the desert, found promising traces of hydrocarbons. Further drilling ensued, and in 1960, a third well on the Murban structure proved the commercial viability of what was to become known as the Bab field, Abu Dhabi's first onshore oil discovery.

Offshore Drilling

Meanwhile, the search for oil had also begun offshore. In 1951, in what was to prove a landmark decision in international law, Sheikh Shakhbut decided to award a separate concession to cover Abu Dhabi's territorial waters outside the three-mile limit. The first concessionaire, an American firm, gave up in 1953, after only a limited exploration effort, a decision they doubtless came to regret. A year later, a new concession was awarded to another firm, D'Arcy Exploration, a subsidiary of BP, later being transferred to Abu Dhabi Marine Areas (ADMA), a joint venture between British Petroleum and Total but later also to have a small Japanese shareholding.

Initial surveys of the seabed promptly began, led by the world-famous French underwater explorer, Commander Jacques-Yves Cousteau. Operating from his research ship, *Calypso,* Cousteau and his team spent a total of 67 days studying the seabed and, on the basis of his findings, ADMA decided to drill a first well at a location known as Umm Shaif.

In 1996, on the occasion of the UAE's Silver Jubilee, and in recognition of his contribution to the country's development, Commander Cousteau was specially decorated by President Sheikh Zayed.

Once again, Abu Dhabi's infant oil industry was at the cutting edge of new technology. A special drilling barge, *ADMA Enterprise,* was constructed in Europe and towed out to the Gulf, where, operating from a base on Das Island, it began work in January 1958. Less than three months later, there was success. The Umm Shaif-1 well struck oil in commercial quantities. The oil era had begun.

Developing the newly discovered fields took time, with the companies and their employees battling onshore against the harsh desert terrain and working against the limits of known technology offshore under the waters of the Gulf. One of the first tasks was to choose suitable sites for terminals from which the oil could be exported. Onshore, a site was selected at Jebel Dhanna, a small hill in the far west, from where oil could flow by gravity into the oil tankers. The painstaking laying of the pipeline across the desert began.

Offshore, Das Island, once only a home for thousands of nesting sea birds, turtles and the occasional fisherman, was selected. At both locations, plants had to be built to treat the oil, as well as accommodation for the workforce, and this took some time to complete. ADMA won the race to build its facilities, and the first cargo of oil from Umm Shaif and Abu Dhabi left from Das in July 1962. The first cargo of crude from the Bab field followed in December 1963.

This was only the start. Onshore, field after field was discovered as exploration continued. The giant Bu Hasa field and the smaller Asab, Sahil and Shah fields followed, all subsequently being brought into production.

A new phase of development is now under way, particularly onshore, with the north-east Bab fields of Rumaitha, Shanayel and Dabb'iya being brought on stream in early 2006 with an installed production capacity of some 110,000 barrels a day, and with Qusaihwira, Bida al-Qemzan and Ruwais, all first discovered in the 1960s and 1970s, scheduled to come into production before 2010. The major Bu Hasa and Bab fields are also being expanded.

Offshore ADMA followed up its success at Umm Shaif by discovering another giant field, Zakum, as well as several smaller ones. The planned relinquishment of some of the concession area later saw several other companies either develop ADMA finds, or make their own discoveries. These included Abu Al Bukhoosh, Mubarraz, Satah and Umm Al Dalkh (all now in production), while a number of other finds have been proven and kept in reserve for the future. Development of several of these is planned during the next few years.

As the industry grew and production expanded, so the political scene in Abu Dhabi changed. In August 1966, Sheikh Zayed succeeded his brother Sheikh Shakhbut as Ruler of Abu Dhabi, becoming President of the new Federation of the United Arab Emirates in 1971.

Joint Ventures

During the next few years, the world's major oil-producing countries – among them the UAE – gradually changed their relationship with the international oil companies, extending their own control over the key, but depletable, resource.

Abu Dhabi – Garden City of the Gulf

Modern methods of seismic surveying unlock the secrets of the desert and enhance Abu Dhabi's future oil reserves.

In Abu Dhabi, this was marked first by the establishment in 1971 of the Abu Dhabi National Oil Company (ADNOC) to represent Government oil interests and to act as owner of an associated resource whose importance was slowly becoming recognized – that of natural gas. The signing of participation agreements with the shareholders in ADPC and ADMA followed, with the Government's percentage in the oil concessions rising in two stages to 60 per cent by the late 1970s. New joint-venture operating companies were formed, ADPC being replaced by the Abu Dhabi Company for Onshore Oil Operations (ADCO) and ADMA by the Abu Dhabi Marine Operating Company (ADMA-OPCO), in both of which the foreign shareholders retained a 40 per-cent stake.

Another joint venture operating firm, the Zakum Development Company (ZADCO), was also set up to operate the reservoirs of the Upper Zakum field, and was later given responsibility for the Umm al-Dalkh and Satah fields. ADNOC originally held 88 per cent of the shares, and the Japan Oil Development Company the remaining 12 per cent, although ADNOC struck a deal with ExxonMobil in 2005 for the US giant to take a 28 per cent share in the Upper Zakum field.

In this process of the Government taking a majority share in the oil concessions, however, the original foreign shareholders in ADPC and ADMA retained a share in the concessions and in the reserves themselves. The approach was unique in the major oil-producing states of the Arabian Gulf, and was adopted by ADNOC and the Government of Abu Dhabi partly to ensure continued access to the very latest in oil industry technological expertise. Over the years, the approach has paid off: Abu Dhabi is now a world leader in techniques such as horizontal drilling and enhanced oil recovery.

The original concession agreements will expire in a few years time, that for the onshore fields by 2014, for example, and ADNOC and its foreign partners are now engaged in negotiations that will lay down the arrangements for future exploitation of the major fields in the years ahead.

A foreign presence is also evident in some of the smaller fields, such as Abu Al Bukhoosh (operated by the French oil company, Total), and Mubarraz, Umm al-Anbar and Neewat al-Ghalan (operated by the Abu Dhabi Oil Company [Japan]), where ADNOC has no shareholding at all. Production levels for these companies, as for the ADNOC Group, are set by the Abu Dhabi Supreme Petroleum Council (SPC), which was established in 1988, and which has been chaired, since its inception, by

The Oil and Gas Sector

Sheikh Khalifa, first as Crown Prince of Abu Dhabi and then, since 2004, as the Ruler. Abu Dhabi's daily production in mid-2007 was around 2.6 million barrels a day, equivalent to the daily quota set for the UAE by the Organization of Petroleum Exporting Countries, OPEC, having risen from some 1.9 million barrels a day in early 2002, in response to increasing world demand.

Installed sustainable production capacity, however, is considerably higher and, by 2010, the UAE as a whole expects to have a sustainable production capacity of more than 3.5 million barrels a day, considerably more than 90 per cent of that being in Abu Dhabi. A target of more than four million barrels a day of capacity is being set for the longer term, although whether or not the necessary investment is actually undertaken may well depend, in part, on the evolution of the balance between global supply and demand.

Overall, investment in Abu Dhabi's oil and gas industry during the next few years is expected to exceed nearly US$22 billion (Dhs 80 billion) during the five year period from 2006-2010, a sure indication of the scale of development being planned.

Naturally, producing oil during more than 40 years has meant that Abu Dhabi's reserves may now be declining, even though there have also been major successes in finding, and then proving up, more reserves to replace those which have been extracted.

An extensive programme of exploration, however, using the very latest techniques to identify oil and gas reservoirs deep beneath the Earth's surface, both onshore and offshore, is continuing to find more reserves to strengthen Abu Dhabi's long-term position as one of the world's major oil producers. There can be few better guarantees of the Emirate's long-term prosperity.

Natural Gas

Together with the oil discoveries have come finds of natural gas, some, but by no means all, of which are associated with oil-bearing reservoirs. At the time that the early oil concession agreements were signed, there was little recognition of the potential importance of natural gas, which was not included. As a result, the gas reserves, whether associated or non-associated, belong in their entirety to the Government of Abu Dhabi.

Until the mid-1970s, virtually all of the associated gas from the oilfields was flared off into the atmosphere, creating the eerie night landscape of flames, once so familiar to visitors arriving in Abu Dhabi by air. At the same time, it polluted the atmosphere and wasted a valuable resource – one estimate suggests that the amount of gas flared in Abu Dhabi from 1973-1976 was worth nearly one billion US dollars.

A programme to end waste was set up in the late 1970s, with the decision by ADNOC – in association with foreign partners, including BP, Shell, Total and Japanese interests – to establish two companies to harness and utilize the associated gas supplies. While some gas is reinjected into the oil reservoirs, to maintain pressure and enhance oil recovery, much is now used for local industry and power and desalination plants and for export.

Onshore, Abu Dhabi Gas Industries Limited (GASCO) was established to handle gas from the ADCO fields, while offshore the Abu Dhabi Gas Liquefaction Company (ADGAS) was created. Both, like ADCO and ADMA-OPCO, are joint ventures between ADNOC and major foreign oil companies.

GASCO and ADCO produce their gas and oil from fields that, for the most part, lie deep in the desert. From there, after initial treatment, it is transferred by a network of pipelines, run by GASCO, to a central point at Habshan, a little north of the growing desert township of Medinat (Bida) Zayed. Here, it is joined by more gas from non-associated fields and reservoirs and further treatment takes place. It is then transferred along more pipelines. One line heads north-east, to Abu Dhabi, where the gas is used for power at the Umm al-Nar industrial complex and power plant, and on further to the world's largest water-desalination and power-generation plant at Taweela, on the coast north-east of Abu Dhabi. A spur line also runs across the desert to the inland oasis-city of Al Ain.

Another extension line runs north-east to Dubai's Jebel Ali industrial zone, helping to provide the power and, through gas-powered desalination plants, the water upon which Dubai's commercial and domestic consumers depend.

The second gas line from Habshan runs north-west to the Ruwais industrial zone, just east of ADCO's oil export terminal at Jebel Dhanna. Here, the clean Natural Gas Liquids (NGLs) are split by a fractionation process into propane, butane and pentane. The bulk of this is then exported, although increasingly it is being put to good use in the local market as, for example, feedstock for petrochemicals.

GASCO, now one of the largest gas-processing companies in the world, is currently engaged in a multi-billion-dollar expansion programme.

The Ruwais zone is the centre of the ADNOC Group's downstream projects. The UAE's largest refinery with a capacity of 420,000 bpd and a 360,000 bpd condensate splitter (both operated by TAKREER, an ADNOC subsidiary), a sulphur plant, a hydrocracker unit, and, largest of all, Borouge, a massive petrochemicals project that came into operation in late 2001 are situated in this zone.

A joint venture between ADNOC and industry leader Borealis, in which the Government of Abu Dhabi has a majority stake through its International Petroleum Investment Company (IPIC), the Borouge plant and associated facilities, completed in 2002, cost US$1.2 billion (Dhs 4.4 billion) to build and is one of the largest polyethylene production facilities in the Middle East. Virtually all of its output is sold overseas. Plans for a major expansion of Borouge operations, to include an even larger petrochemicals complex, are under way and will involve an investment of a further US$2.5 billion (Dhs 9 billion) and are scheduled to be completed by 2010.

Offshore, ADGAS and ADMA-OPCO share facilities on Das Island. Here, gas from the offshore oilfields is collected and treated, producing Liquefied Natural Gas (LNG), and Liquefied Petroleum Gas (LPG). Initially, the plant had a capacity of two million tonnes a year (t/y) of LNG and 500,000 t/y of LPG, all of the LNG and most of the LPG being exported to Japan, under a long-term contract with the Tokyo Electric Power Company (TEPCO).

Rising demand from Japan and the opening up of new markets has resulted in the plant has been enlarged several times and total capacity is now around 7.7 million t/y of LNG and nearly three million t/y of LPG. Feedstock for the plants comes from the ADMA-OPCO, ZADCO and Abu al-Bukhoosh fields.

With the increasing demand for gas both as feedstock for plants in the Ruwais zone and for fuel for industries and other consumers elsewhere in the UAE, planning is now under way for a major gas pipeline to link up the offshore and onshore gas fields to bring further integration into Abu Dhabi's gas industry. Indeed, the projected increase during the next few years in demand for gas in Abu Dhabi, and in the rest of the UAE, is so great that the focus of the hydrocarbons industry is likely to switch from oil to gas, though expansion of oil production capacity will also demand heavy investment. There are also multi-billion dollar plans to develop sour gas reserves in Abu Dhabi's onshore Shah and Bab fields, scheduled to get under way in 2008.

As the range of products from the ADNOC Group has grown, so it has been obliged to diversify. From the mid-1970s, for example, its majority shareholding in the oil concessions gave ADNOC its own crude oil to market. The rapid expansion of the local economy and the building and subsequent expansion of refineries first at Umm al-Nar, and then Ruwais, provided a captive and growing local market for refined fuels. Operated by ADNOC subsidiary TAKREER, the refineries now have a capacity to process nearly a million barrels a day of oil and condensate.

Plans were also announced in 2007 for the construction of an oil pipeline from Habshan, in Abu Dhabi, to the UAE East Coast port of Fujairah, where another refinery will also be built, this time by the Government-owned International Petroleum Investment Company, IPIC.

Through its wholly owned subsidiary the Abu Dhabi National Oil Company for Distribution (ADNOC-FOD), which operates in the northern emirates as well as in Abu Dhabi, ADNOC also supplies fuel for household use, for cars, for planes and for shipping.

Despite the growth in this home-based demand, ADNOC has millions of barrels of crude oil a year available for export, primarily on long-term contracts. Rather than rely entirely on chartering tankers, ADNOC created its own shipping firm, the Abu Dhabi National Tanker Company (ADNATCO), whose fleet of seven tankers carries ADNOC oil to markets around the world.

The establishment of the gas industry required yet more ships. The Natural Gas Shipping Company (NGSCO), is responsible for the shipment of LNG from the ADGAS facility on Das Island, and now operates eight of the largest gas carriers in the world.

Industry Expansion

The ADNOC Group also comprises a number of other firms, some of which have grown to become industry leaders. These include Irshad, which handles the export terminals; Abu Dhabi Drilling and Chemical Products Company (ADDCAP), manufacturing chemicals for the industry; National Marine Services; the National Drilling Company, one of the largest drilling firms in the Middle East; and Ruwais Fertilizer Industries (FERTIL), which exports its products around the world.

A particular success has been the National Petroleum Construction Company (NPCC) that not only builds offshore jackets and platforms for installation in Abu Dhabi's oilfields, but has also won contracts to build massive structures for other countries, including India and Iran. It started life as a member of the ADNOC Group, but has now been transferred to a government holding company, prior to being privatized, a first step along the road of inviting private investors into the local oil and gas industry.

As the economy of Abu Dhabi grows, and becomes more sophisticated, further privatization may well occur. In the meantime, a group of Abu Dhabi businessmen, including a former chief executive officer of ADNOC, have successfully established their own firm, Aabar Petroleum Investment Company, the first firm of its type in the Gulf to be quoted on the stock market. Starting with interests in the oil-services industry in the UAE, it rapidly branched out, and purchased a Singapore-based oil and gas producer in early 2006. More acquisitions are expected.

Another major component of Abu Dhabi's burgeoning oil and gas industry is Dolphin Energy, whose majority shareholder is the Mubadala Development Company, a holding company for the Government of Abu Dhabi, with Occidental Petroleum and Total as foreign minority shareholders. Dolphin's basic objective is to transport gas from Qatar's huge offshore North Field to a landfall near Taweela, making Abu Dhabi the centre of a new regional network.

The initial planned capacity of the pipeline is two billion standard cubic feet of gas a day, for supply to major industrial users such as the Abu Dhabi Water and

Abu Dhabi – Garden City of the Gulf

Clearing old equipment and a zero-flare policy has allowed the desert to return to its natural splendour and plants such as the desert squash, *Citrullus colocynthis* (above), and the Sodom's apple, *Calotropis procera* (opposite), to thrive.

Electricity Authority and the Dubai Supply Authority and, eventually it is hoped, to customers further afield. Dolphin is also supplying gas from Oman, via Al Ain, to the Qidfa power and desalination plant in Fujairah, although when the available supplies from Oman are depleted, Dolphin will then become a major supplier to Oman as well.

From the initial base of the production of crude oil, the Abu Dhabi oil industry has expanded and diversified so that the production of oil itself, though key to the whole process, now represents the core of an industrial and transportation sector that includes gas production, petrochemicals, heavy engineering, shipping and distribution – an integrated industry that is the powerhouse of Abu Dhabi's economy.

Effect on the Environment

The oil and gas industry is one that recognizes a responsibility to the future of Abu Dhabi extending beyond that of simply providing the financial resources that underpin and make possible its continued growth.

During the early phase of the discovery and development of the fields and then of the massive growth that saw ADNOC emerge as one of the largest integrated oil and gas producing companies in the world, the priorities were those of growth itself. One consequence was that, in Abu Dhabi as elsewhere, the industry was responsible for a significant degree of environmental pollution. In the deserts and offshore, equipment that had been cast aside left its mark, while the flaring of the associated gas from the oilfields had a massive, if largely

unrecognized, impact upon the atmosphere. The picture began to change in the mid-1970s. The value of natural gas as a clean fuel began to be widely recognized, and it became apparent that the flaring represented not simply the burning of a non-renewable resource, but the burning of money as well.

At the same time, there was the gradual emergence at a global level of a greater degree of environmental consciousness. Abu Dhabi was not immune. The UAE's first voluntary environmental organization, the Emirates Natural History Group, was formed in 1977, and promptly attracted long-term support from the oil companies, a relationship that continues until today.

During the last few years, the ADNOC Group has devised and implemented one of the toughest environmental-protection programmes found within the oil industry, both offshore and onshore.

ADNOC has shown that it is also prepared to make a direct choice between the development of oil production and conservation of the environment. Studies of atmospheric emissions in the late 1990s showed that some 70 per cent of the emissions came from a few small offshore fields. In what is perhaps a first for the Arabian Gulf, one small offshore field was taken out of production in the late 1990s simply because it was decided that the expenditure necessary to bring the field's environmental performance up to acceptable standards would deprive it of its commercial viability.

In some other small fields, operated by the Abu Dhabi Oil Company (Japan), a multi-million dollar programme for the reinjection of sour and acid gas was implemented. As a result, not only has flaring of emissions been virtually eliminated, but the rate of oil recovery from the field has increased, evidence that a responsible environmental approach can have a profitable outcome as well.

The development of a number of other offshore discoveries has also been postponed because of the potential adverse environmental impact.

Millions of dollars have been spent on cleaning up the waste from a previous, less enlightened period, while the flaring of natural gas has been steadily reduced during the last few years, with a 'zero-flaring' target being set.

The maturity of Abu Dhabi's oil industry has also meant that many of the older installations, particularly offshore, are reaching the end of their working life. As part of a campaign to rehabilitate the seabed, rigs, well-heads and production platforms that are scheduled for de-commissioning are now being converted into artificial reefs where fish can safely breed. All this is expensive, of course, but these moves are not only important in terms of their environmental impact, but are also necessary for the development of the industry.

As the economy of Abu Dhabi, and the UAE as a whole has continued to expand and to diversify away from dependence on oil, so the sector's share of Gross Domestic Product has continued to decline. More than two thirds in the 1970s, it has fallen over the years to less than a third for the country as a whole, although the sharp upturn in world oil prices from 2005 into late 2007 saw the share increasing once again. Although its contribution varies because of the vagaries of international oil prices, the underlying trend remains firmly downwards.

Yet the industry remains central to the economy, partly because of the employment, construction and engineering projects related to it, all of which stimulate expenditure in other sectors but, more crucially, because it continues to provide the bulk of the income received by the Government, which is then invested in other parts of the economy.

While some of the major projects in other spheres, such as construction, transport and tourism, are likely to grab the headlines in the years ahead, the role of the oil and gas industry, both upstream and, increasingly, downstream, will continue to underpin Abu Dhabi's enviable prosperity.

Chapter Six
A Green and Pleasant Emirate

A first-time visitor to the Emirate of Abu Dhabi may well arrive with a mental image of kilometres upon kilometres of rolling and barren sand dunes, interspersed with only the occasional oasis of palm trees. Such an impression can be forgiven for, after all, Abu Dhabi does lie in desert Arabia, on the edge of the great Rub al-Khali, or the Empty Quarter, one of the most arid environments on earth.

This image, though, was never completely accurate, and is far from true today. During the course of the last four decades, Abu Dhabi has seen the implementation of one of the world's most extensive programmes of afforestation and agricultural development, with more than 100 million forest trees, and a further 40 million or so date palms, being planted across the wastes of the desert, covering an area of some 200,000 hectares. At the same time, the major urban centres have been well supplied with lavish parks and gardens, while rows of trees line the highways through the desert, providing both a touch of green against the sandy coloured wastes, and barriers to hold back the movement of the shifting sands.

It is little wonder then that the city of Abu Dhabi itself has earned the nickname of 'Garden City of the Gulf' and that the Emirate as a whole now has a thriving

Abu Dhabi Corniche has enjoyed extensive changes during the past 35 years, with the construction of iconic buildings such as the Abu Dhabi Investment Authority Building.

Abu Dhabi – Garden City of the Gulf

Despite its modern buildings, Abu Dhabi is also a city of parks and fountains where millions have been invested in a greening programme.

agricultural sector on what was once nothing but arid sand or gravel plains.

In a land such as Abu Dhabi, where rainfall is scanty and unpredictable and where there is not a single natural stream or river, it is not surprising that one of the dreams of its people has been that of waving fields of crops, of forests and gardens, and of lush greenery that nature itself does not provide. During the course of the last 40 years or so, great strides have been made towards turning that dream into reality.

The driving force behind the afforestation and agricultural programme, as with so many other aspects of the Emirate's development, was former Abu Dhabi Ruler and UAE President, Sheikh Zayed, who died in late 2004. Partly brought up in the inland oasis of Al Ain, he became Ruler's Representative there in 1946, marking the beginning of what became more than half a century in Government.

One of his earliest tasks was to revive agriculture in the area. He achieved this

Bougainvillea, a firm favourite throughout the Emirates, never fails to add a splash of colour to Abu Dhabi's verdant parks and gardens.

by arranging for some of the old *falaj* underground water channels to be cleaned out and repaired so that they would flow again, and also arranged for a new *falaj* to be dug, the first for many years. Eager to ensure that the valuable resources of water were shared fairly, he revised the ancient system of water distribution, and ordered that henceforth farmers in the oasis should have access to the water they needed without charge. Not surprisingly, the agricultural sector of Al Ain's economy promptly took a turn for the better.

At the same time, Sheikh Zayed also set out deliberately, and with forethought, to plan for the long-term beautification of what, at the time, was nothing more than a cluster of six little villages of mud-brick houses surrounded by palm groves and scrub. During the 1950s, he commenced the planting of tender saplings along the edges of dusty sandy tracks. Today those saplings, now great avenues of trees, line the modern highways of the city of Al Ain, making the city one of the greenest in Arabia.

Afforestation

When Sheikh Zayed became Ruler of Abu Dhabi in 1966, he expanded the tree-planting programme to cover the whole of the Emirate. Out in the deserts, once home to only the occasional hardy *ghaf* and acacia, vast areas are covered by tree plantations, some relatively small, while others cover hundreds or even thousands of hectares – serried ranks of vegetation stretching away as far as the eye can see. Amid the modern buildings of the cities and towns, well-planted parks offer 'green lungs' that would be the envy of many other countries. They are not merely relaxing to the eye but also provide venues for leisure and recreation that are eagerly sought after, especially during the cooler months of the year. It has, by any standards, been a truly remarkable achievement.

The process of afforestation and the reclamation of land for agriculture has been given a significant boost in recent years by the ready availability of desalinated water, a by-product of electricity generation.

At the same time, however, there has been a growing recognition of the need to ensure that wastage of water is kept to a minimum.

Virtually all of the sewage and other wastewater from the city of Abu Dhabi is, for example, recycled and is then used for the irrigation of parks and gardens. Detailed studies of the desert tree plantations have been undertaken to ensure that the supply of irrigation water is sufficient, but not in excess, to encourage

Abu Dhabi – Garden City of the Gulf

Abu Dhabi has a number of cool, decorative fountains that enhance its many green areas.

the trees, wherever possible, to extend their own root systems so that they can tap into the natural supplies of water underground.

With the rapidly burgeoning demand for water for other uses, in industry and for the fast-growing population of Abu Dhabi, however, there has been a marked decline in the underground water table during the past few decades, and even with the construction of massive new water-desalination and power-generation plants has the supply only just being keeping up with demand.

One aspect of the recent restructuring of the Government of Abu Dhabi has been the placing of the Emirate's forests under the control of the Environment Agency – Abu Dhabi (EAD), which is now looking both at controlling the use of water more effectively and at the long-term sustainability of the forestry programme. There has been a slowing down in the rate of new planting, while the forests that have been successfully established in the past will now be obliged, wherever possible, to survive on available ground-water supplies, with a long-term phased reduction in the rate of increase in irrigation water.

That process will not have any effect on the planting of parks and gardens and along the highways. Deep in the deserts, though, the preparation of new land for tree planting has come to a halt, leaving much of the land as rolling sand dunes, as it has been for thousands of years.

A similar drive to eliminate wastage and to increase efficiency is also under way in the Emirate's agricultural sector.

Contrary to the popular but erroneously held image of the UAE, the Emirate of Abu Dhabi has always had some agriculture. In the Al Ain oasis, the tapping of underground resources by wells and, since around 1000 BC, by *falaj* underground water channels, has permitted farming for at least 5,000 years, while in the great arc of the Liwa Oasis in the south, small palm groves have always been able to survive, thanks to the trapping of small underground reservoirs of fresh water at the base of the great sand dunes.

A Green and Pleasant Emirate

With its lavish parks and gardens, Abu Dhabi has been called the 'Garden City of the Gulf'.

Now, however, agricultural production has expanded, thanks in no small measure to the ready availability of government assistance for farmers. Such assistance can include the preparation of farm land, the drilling of water wells or laying of pipes to bring in desalinated water, and then the handing over, completely free of charge, of a farm ready for cultivation.

The help continues, with the provision of seeds and fertilizers at a subsidized rate, and a guaranteed government purchase scheme for crops for those farmers who wish to take advantage of it. Not surprisingly, the growth in agricultural production has been substantial, and the Emirate now has more than 20,000 farms.

The majority of these are in the Eastern Region, in the vicinity of Al Ain, but also stretching southwards towards Umm az-Zamul, where Oman, Saudi Arabia and the UAE meet on the edge of the Rub al-Khali; and along the highways running from Al Ain north to Dubai and westwards to Abu Dhabi. Others can be found in the Western Region, particularly in the Liwa Oases, and lining the road running north-east from Abu Dhabi towards the Dubai border at Saih ash Shaib.

Many of the farms are small, cultivated by their owners to provide food for domestic consumption, but there are other, larger enterprises, that produce crops for the market. More than two million tonnes of vegetables are now produced every year, an impressive total for an agricultural sector that can rarely count upon the blessing of rainfall. The most popular crops are tomatoes and cabbages, although other crops such as potatoes have also been successfully introduced.

Dates are another important crop, with more than 40 million date palms having been planted in the UAE as a whole, the vast majority in Abu Dhabi, and the country is now one of the largest producers of dates in the world. Some of the dates themselves are for the farmers' own consumption, while several thousand tonnes a year are processed and packed for local supermarkets or for export. Nevertheless, dates on trees by the roadside or in the parks in the towns and cities can be freely collected and eaten by anyone.

Abu Dhabi – Garden City of the Gulf

Animal husbandry has not been neglected, with total livestock including more than 200,000 camels, nearly a million goats and sheep, and more than 20,000 cattle, many of which are found in modern dairy farms, producing milk and other products for local consumers. Poultry farming has been successful too, with more than 100 million eggs a year being produced.

In the era before oil, there were natural controls on the amount of livestock roaming across the desert for grazing. After good rainfall, there was plenty to eat, and herds grew, but during the frequent droughts, many animals died of thirst or starvation. After the beginning of modern development, though, access to 4x4 vehicles and to water and food supplies that could be transported on the back of a truck meant that livestock numbers grew, encouraged by a programme of government subsidies.

While this meant that there was a marked increase in the total number of livestock, it also meant that the desert rangelands were over-grazed, with a consequent, and damaging effect on the natural vegetation.

Following prompting from the EAD, new legislation was introduced in early 2006 to regulate grazing and to cut back on the subsidies, the hope being that this would lead to a reduction in livestock numbers so that the desert vegetation could regenerate. The conservation of the natural environment, and of its plants, animals and birds, is being given a high priority.

Natural Environment

To the casual observer, it may seem as though Abu Dhabi's natural environment is relatively uninteresting – there are sand dunes, salt flats, coastal beaches with the occasional stand of mangroves, but certainly no great natural forests or waving prairies. The climate, of course, precludes this: plant and animal life has to struggle to survive in the harsh desert and semi-desert. Indeed, the very nature of this environment means that the survival of wildlife is often balanced on a

> Nearly a million goats and sheep are estimated to occur in the Emirate's many smallholdings.

A Green and Pleasant Emirate

precarious knife-edge, where even a limited amount of human impact can have a devastating effect.

The surface geology of Abu Dhabi, in effect the scenery itself, has a beauty of its own, while it is also of considerable scientific interest. The *sabkha* salt flats, which stretch from north-east of Abu Dhabi all along the coastline to the Sila'a area, in the extreme west, are the largest of their kind in the world, and have provided geological information of international importance. Some can also be found far inland.

The great sand dunes of the Liwa area are up to 100 metres high, with gravel or salt-flat plains lying between them. Comprising the north-east edge of the Empty Quarter or Rub al-Khali, they are also important examples of the type. Anyone who has seen the dunes in the dawn or dusk light will be able to testify that they can, indeed, have a beauty and grandeur all of their own.

The only real mountain within the territory of Abu Dhabi, the great whaleback of Jebel Hafit, just south of Al Ain, which rises some 1,000 metres above sea level, has been carved by the forces of nature over millions of years into often fantastical shapes, while fossils millions of years old can be found within its rocks. From the top of the mountain, on a clear day, you can look out for miles over the city of Al Ain or out across the adjacent deserts. Deep inside the mountain are long caves carved out by water action in the past, although these are inaccessible except with special permission.

The coasts and the islands of the Emirate have their own importance too, although most of the latter are off-limits to casual visitors, while offshore on the seabed there are millions of pearl oysters, harvested for thousands of years by local inhabitants until a few decades ago. In the waters of the Arabian Gulf, several species of turtle and dolphin and the endangered dugong, or 'sea cow,' can be found, as well as an occasional whale for the lucky observer.

The great sand dunes of the Empty Quarter have a grandeur and beauty all of their own.

Wildlife Protection

Within the landscape and seascape is a multitude of fascinating wildlife, much of it being the object of study by EAD, formerly known as the Environmental Research and Wildlife Development Agency (ERWDA), and by members of voluntary organizations such as the Emirates Natural History Group, now 30 years old, and the Emirates Bird Records Committee, which maintains the official list of bird species seen in the country.

With President HH Sheikh Khalifa bin Zayed Al Nahyan as its Honorary Chairman, and with Deputy Prime Minister HE Sheikh Hamdan bin Zayed Al Nahyan as its Chairman, EAD is charged with both studying and protecting the wildlife of the Emirate – not just plants and animals, but also the surroundings in which they live.

It is, for example, studying the gentle dugong, a marine mammal that's said to be at the origin of the legend of the mermaid. Abu Dhabi's offshore waters are home to the second-largest population of dugongs in the world. In addition, EAD has also launched a study of marine turtles, involving the plotting of their nesting sites on offshore islands and the tagging of some turtles with small transmitters so that their movements can be tracked by satellite.

Other marine projects have included the tagging of sailfish, a detailed study of the fishery resources of Abu Dhabi's waters and, in collaboration with the World Wide Fund for Nature (WWF) and local sponsor Dolphin Energy, a major review of coral reefs – one of the key indicators of the health of the marine environment.

Another body to have undertaken important scientific research on the coast and islands is the Emirates Heritage Club, whose Department of Environmental Research has produced a detailed Marine Atlas of Abu Dhabi that provides a useful baseline study against which future changes in marine life can be measured.

Onshore, EAD and other scientists are engaged in studies of the plants of the desert and of some of the animals that live among them, such as the desert hare, of which at least two sub-species are present, and a host of lizards and smaller animals. A key focus of its work is the study of the houbara bustard, the favoured quarry of local falconers, and of saker and peregrine falcons. One of the objectives is to develop a large-scale captive breeding programme as part of efforts to conserve all three species in the wild and successful experiments at releasing houbara into Abu Dhabi's deserts have already got under way.

EAD is also responsible for the designation and management of protected areas. The first Marine Protected Area (MPA), covering more than 4,000 square kilometres of inshore waters around the island of Marawah, as well as this and other smaller islands, was formally designated in early 2002, while the second MPA, covering nearly 500 square kilometres around the Yasat islands, in the far west of Abu Dhabi, was formally designated in late 2005. A third, smaller, area, just west of Abu Dhabi island, was designated in 2006. In these areas, fishing is tightly controlled and populations of turtles, dugongs and seabirds are strictly protected, giving Abu Dhabi's wildlife a chance to recover from over-exploitation.

EAD is also charged with the responsibility for monitoring and protecting the environment throughout the Emirate, and has been given tough regulatory powers that assign to it the responsibility for permits for new development. This is done only after the appropriate Environmental Impact Assessments or Environmental Baseline Studies have been carried out. While property developers and others may find their projects are delayed or revised as a result of not being able to meet EAD's demands, this all contributes to a more effective conservation of the environment for the years ahead, from which all of the inhabitants of the Emirate will benefit.

Mangroves – a good indicator of the quality of the environment where they occur – are still a common sight along Abu Dhabi's coast.

Abu Dhabi – Garden City of the Gulf

Arabian oryx have been released into the remote desert areas of Abu Dhabi, along with sand and mountain gazelle.

Though details such as these may be little noticed by many of Abu Dhabi's inhabitants, or by its visitors, the policy of environmental protection implemented by Government means, of course, that there is much more to see in the way of wildlife and nature.

Among the most easily visible wildlife in Abu Dhabi is the bird population. Studies by members of the Emirates Bird Records Committee and other ornithologists have shown that more than a hundred species of birds breed in the Emirates, many of them in Abu Dhabi.

Offshore islands such as Qarnein and Dayyinah, for example, are the home during the summer breeding season to colonies of thousands of sea birds. Qarnein, indeed, provided with special protection by Sheikh Hamdan bin Zayed, is one of the most important sites for breeding birds anywhere in the whole of Arabia. It has now been designated as a 'Gift to the Earth' under a programme designed by the World Wide Fund for Nature (WWF) to preserve some of the world's best nature reserves for all time.

Besides the breeding birds, there are the passage migrants, hundreds of thousands of which pass across Abu Dhabi every year during their migration from breeding grounds in Siberia to wintering grounds in Africa. Tens of thousands of birds choose to stay over in Abu Dhabi, and key wetland sites such as the Dabb'iya Peninsula and the island of Marawah, west of Abu Dhabi, and the Al Wathba Lakes (an EAD-managed nature sanctuary approximately 40 kilometres inland from Abu Dhabi), can, at their peak, hold several thousand birds.

Even in the city itself, there are important sites for birds, such as the mangrove-lined Eastern Lagoon on the eastern side of the island, important for sea birds and waders, and the Ra's al-Akhdar headland at the north-western tip, which regularly produces rare species of migrants and also has a number of breeding species.

During the course of the last few years, the UAE has begun to attract visitors from overseas who come with the specific intention of looking at the country's varied birdlife. Of the 420 or so species of birds recorded in the UAE, more than 75 per cent have been seen on the island of Abu Dhabi itself. Probably no other major city in the world can offer such a large percentage of a country's bird list.

The conservation of the environment, both on land and offshore, and of the wildlife to be found within it, has long been a part of Government policy. Hunting of wildlife was, for example, banned throughout the Emirate in 1977, while tough new environmental legislation, applicable throughout the Emirates, provides protection for virtually all of the country's wildlife.

The original policy was first devised by Sheikh Zayed, who himself showed the way by creating an impressive collection of endangered wildlife on the western island of Sir Bani Yas. Its focus is on species native to the UAE, such as the Arabian oryx and sand and mountain gazelles, and those indigenous to other desert and semi-desert areas, such as the scimitar-horned oryx and the addax.

The latter two species are both from Africa and are under serious threat, if not actually extinct, in the wild, and the collection is of international importance. Release programmes for Arabian oryx and both sand and mountain gazelles have been started in the desert regions of Abu Dhabi, and the lucky explorer venturing out into the remoter regions may well be rewarded by a glimpse of these animals, which once roamed free in large numbers through the landscape.

Much of the country's landscape and wildlife is difficult to access or hard to see, but quite a lot is easy to visit and simple to spot, whether in and around the cities of Abu Dhabi and Al Ain, or along the highways that traverse the desert. Those who keep their eyes open will swiftly find the whole of the Emirate of Abu Dhabi a fascinating and remarkable place.

Dangerous but beautiful, the scorpion *Apistobuthus pterygocercus* is encountered in the sand dunes of the Rub al-Khali.

Abu Dhabi – Garden City of the Gulf

Chapter Seven
Abu Dhabi's Leisure Industry

> A number of adventure companies offer exciting guided safaris into the desert interior.

There's been a tremendous growth in Western-style sport and leisure activities since oil first started flowing from Abu Dhabi's wells in the early 1960s. This growth was caused both by the influx of expatriates already familiar with such sports and by the interest shown by the local population in non traditional sports. The upshot was an astonishing range and quality of sports facilities and a booming leisure industry that benefits from almost perfect weather conditions for nearly eight months of the year. Nevertheless, despite this scenario, traditional Arab sports have flourished.

Falconry and camel racing, for example, have always been linked to the Gulf states. Before the discovery of oil, these two activities were deeply rooted in the indigenous way of life, but both activities have now become fully fledged sports in their own right.

Although falcons are no longer used except for sport, falconry, known as the 'sport of sheikhs', is still a symbol of national cultural identity and is becoming ever more popular with local enthusiasts. Visitors can enjoy falconry displays, at Al Ain Zoo, for example, that highlight the speed and precision of these noble birds of prey and even have the chance to try the sport.

The Arabian dromedary, once an essential means of transport for the Bedouins and today largely replaced by 4x4s, still features in camel races. The one-humped camel remains a source of pride for owners who partake in races and considerable time and money is invested in these animals. Winners may be as pampered as

racing Thoroughbred horses. Races are held during winter weekends and on public holidays at the Al Wathba Camel Racetrack, 45 kilometres outside Abu Dhabi, and at Al Ain Camel Racetrack, as well as at other smaller tracks in the Western Region. These provide visitors with an opportunity to see this ancient and highly competitive sport at close quarters. There's much friendly rivalry among camel owners, and big prizes are at stake. Spectators are virtually guaranteed a memorable experience, particularly since the owners cruise alongside the racetrack in their 4x4s beside their galloping entries, adding to the busy, colourful atmosphere. One recently introduced feature, an example of the way in which Abu Dhabi offers an intriguing mixture of the traditional and the modern, is the replacement of young jockeys by radio-controlled robots.

Besides watching camel racing, visitors can also enjoy riding camels at certain heritage sites and on desert safaris organized by Abu Dhabi's tour companies. They can also visit the camel market in Al Ain.

Desert trips may include a barbecue, camel rides, belly dancing and even a night under canvas.

Abu Dhabi – Garden City of the Gulf

Abu Dhabi's history is linked not only to the desert but also to the sea – a tie still widely celebrated on national and religious holidays with picturesque sailing and rowing races off the Abu Dhabi Corniche or Al Raha Beach near Al Maqta'a Bridge. The rowing races on these occasions are not to be missed, if only to admire the beauty of the dark, slender boats gliding through the turquoise waters and hear the chanting of the oarsmen. The oarsmen arrive from all over the Emirates to compete both for cash prizes and for the honour of their team. Each traditional hand-made teak boat is manned by between 70 and 150 oarsmen (although there are also smaller classes) and the preparations and post-race celebrations are colourful spectacles of local traditions.

Contrary to most people's predictions, the sailing dhow hasn't vanished from local waters and it too is enjoying a period of renaissance, albeit for reasons of sport rather than trade. There can be few more thrilling sights than to watch elegant full-sized racing dhows competing in the annual regattas, their white sails billowing in the wind.

But other, more modern, sports also enjoy their share of popularity. The International Marine Sports Club on the Abu Dhabi breakwater has become a leading centre for Formula One Offshore powerboat racing. The international season runs from February to December and ends with a final round hosted in Abu Dhabi. The UAE is represented by the Emirates Formula One Team, the first team from the Arab World to participate in these races.

Formula One motor racing will also make its debut in Abu Dhabi in early 2009, with the holding of the first Abu Dhabi Formula One Grand Prix on a specially built track on Yas Island, close to Abu Dhabi, where a 'Ferrari Theme Park' is also under construction in collaboration with the Italian car manufacturer.

This proliferation of sports was not always so. Little more than 40 years ago, when virtually the only expatriates in Abu Dhabi were those involved in oil exploration or in small-scale business, sports facilities were negligible. But, once the oil boom took off, both government and private sectors were quick to

Below: A UIM Class Two powerboat from the prize-winning Victory Team shows its paces in a race organized by the Abu Dhabi International Marine Club.

Opposite page: A crew of traditional rowers training off the Corniche.

Abu Dhabi – Garden City of the Gulf

Fishing for hammour (rock cod), red snapper, barracuda, kingfish and sailfish is a perfect way to spend a day out on the Arabian Gulf.

respond to the need for a leisure industry. Land and support was given for the construction of sports clubs, and hotel chains were encouraged to set up in Abu Dhabi and provide further venues tailored primarily for the expatriate community.

The spectacular Zayed Sports City on the Western Road is a measure of Abu Dhabi's commitment to providing the best facilities for the country's youth, its huge vaulted silhouette housing the latest facilities for football and other major sports events. As in most parts of the world, football is the most popular national sport – particularly among local youth – and the country boasts a thriving league and cup competition in which Abu Dhabi clubs dominate. The Abu Dhabi Cricket Council's modern US$15 million (Dhs 55 million) stadium is another example of the Emirate's determination to become a global sporting capital.

For a large number of Abu Dhabi residents, and for the ever-increasing number of tourists, most leisure activities, especially water sports, are centred on the city's hotels. The major hotels, resorts and beach clubs are all equipped with extensive recreational club facilities and private beaches.

The climate of Abu Dhabi, with only a few days in midwinter being marred by stormy weather and rain, is ideal for outdoor sports of all types, except in the torrid heat of summer. The spring and autumn months, in particular, promise comfortable temperatures ranging from 20°C to 30°C and water sports, with the good winds and calm, warm waters around Abu Dhabi island, have flourished. Jet-skiing (particularly fashionable among young UAE citizens), water-skiing, sail-boarding, kite-boarding, canoeing and kayaking are all popular. Sailing enthusiasts, too, have a wide choice, although smaller dinghy sailing has largely been eclipsed by the excitement of more speedy catamarans.

The InterContinental Hotel, the International Marine and Sports Club and Abu Dhabi Marina & Yacht Club have marinas, resplendent with motor launches and yachts of every size and description. The sheltered waters and surrounding islands make Abu Dhabi a safe and exciting playground for powerboat enthusiasts, many of whom own their own craft.

During the weekends water-skiers and anglers take to the seas in droves – fishing for sailfish, kingfish, queenfish, dorado, red snapper, *shari* and the local favourite, *hammour* (rock cod). A number of hotels have their own sport-fishing boats and tackle and will customize trips to suit guests' wishes.

For many, this is a perfect way to spend a day – others may prefer to explore Abu Dhabi's islands and the more adventurous can even arrange to be dropped off at a secluded island for an overnight stay. Dhows are available for hire by the half-day, full-day or evening, and barbecues on the beach are popular.

The Emirate's coastline is punctuated by more than 100 islands (including Abu Dhabi island itself), most of which are flat, sandy and uninhabited. Island hopping is a popular activity and destinations include Lulu Island, a large man-made island just off the Abu Dhabi Corniche; Saadiyat Island, soon to be transformed into a major tourism hub; Futaisi Island; and Sir Bani Yas Island, 250 kilometres to the west of Abu Dhabi. Bahrani and 'Cut' islands are also popular getaways.

Dhow cruises along the Abu Dhabi Corniche are also popular and a buffet or full meal can be arranged. As an alternative to a dhow, modern motor cruisers take passengers on evening cruises along the Corniche, or can be chartered by individuals or parties. Enjoying a fine meal and friendly atmosphere while watching the sun set over the water is an experience to remember.

Many leading hotels have temperature-controlled swimming pools and scuba-diving courses, dive boats and diving equipment are all available, leading to internationally recognized certification such as those of the PADI (Professional Association of Diving Instructors) organization.

The local waters enjoy a variety of marine life, and it's possible to dive all year round in the warm sea. Many good dive sites are easily accessible from Abu Dhabi, including wreck or deep-water dives. Visitors may also venture to the east coast to dive in the Gulf of Oman, and further north to explore the Musandam Peninsula. Abu Dhabi's diving companies organize all manner of trips from recreational snorkelling to technical diving.

In a constant battle to outdo each other, the recreation and health clubs offer an astonishing array of sports and leisure opportunities, ranging from paragliding and banana-boat rides to squash and salsa classes. Gymnasiums are fully equipped with state-of-the-art exercise machines and offer training courses such as weight loss or bodybuilding. Those seeking a more relaxed approach can sink into a Jacuzzi, soak in a sauna or steam room, or take in some *shiatsu* or Chinese massage, followed by an aromatherapy session. Abu Dhabi is certainly a tremendous place to take up a new hobby or sport, as various clubs offer classes as diverse as horse-riding, karate, ballet, *t'ai chi*, jazz dance and aerobics.

Tennis, the perfect social game, remains a firm favourite, with tournaments and competitions for all levels and ages. The Abu Dhabi Health and Fitness Club runs its own tennis academy, and floodlit courts make it possible to play in the relative cool of the summer evenings. Another popular racquet sport, particularly during the hot and humid summer months, is squash, played on air-conditioned courts.

Not all clubs are based in hotels. There are many clubs for the different nationalities among the expatriate workforce and larger, more established companies often provide recreational facilities for their employees. One of the oldest, independent establishments is known simply as The Club, sometimes erroneously referred to as the British Club, although it attracts members of every nationality for its social, sporting and cultural activities. The Abu Dhabi Marina & Yacht Club has also become a popular venue among expatriates as well as well-travelled visitors.

Abu Dhabi – Garden City of the Gulf

Abu Dhabi has hosted many international polo teams and the Emirate is a major contributor to the domestic circuit.

The Tourist Club, which gave its name to an area on the north-east of Abu Dhabi island, is now demolished but the ice-skating rink at Zayed Sports City can accommodate 450 skaters and 1,200 spectators, and is the regular venue for Emirati and expatriate ice-hockey teams.

Ghantoot is the home of the Ghantoot Racing & Polo Club, the first floodlit polo club in Abu Dhabi Emirate. It has hosted many international teams and has become a major contributor to the domestic polo circuit.

Foremost among desert activities has to be off-road driving, where motoring enthusiasts head out in 4x4 vehicles to explore the desert wilderness. Novices are advised always to travel in convoys, as it's easy to get stuck in the soft sand or lost in the desert. For those who feel happier in the hands of professionals, a number of adventure-travel companies offer guided desert safaris. Such trips may include an Arabian barbecue, a camel ride, belly dancing and even a night under canvas. As a direct offshoot of these desert safaris, sand-skiing was introduced as an exhilarating sport on the steep slopes of the splendid orange-red dunes of Liwa Oasis and Al Ain, among the tallest in the world.

On a less slippery and more genteel note, there's golf. Traditionally, the game here was played on sand where, in order to simulate the grass game as much as possible, players hit the ball off a piece of Astroturf – except when on the compacted sand greens, better known as 'browns'. However, in recent years, world-class facilities have been introduced to the Emirate.

Created majestically out of the *sabkha* (salt flats) just off Abu Dhabi island, the Abu Dhabi Golf Club by Sheraton, 20 minutes from the city centre, features one 18-hole course and one nine-hole course. The par 72 National Course provides a rewarding challenge for even the most skilled golfers while the nine hole, par 36, Garden Course is more forgiving, making it ideal for all levels of player. Extensive practice facilities include an 18-hole putting green, chipping greens, practice bunkers, and the largest driving range in the Gulf. The club's leisure facilities include a sports club, an outdoor free-form swimming pool, a well-equipped gymnasium, four floodlit tennis courts, two glass-back squash courts, a health club (with spa, sauna, steam room, Jacuzzi and locker rooms), and restaurants in the clubhouse.

The Abu Dhabi Golf and Equestrian Club has a floodlit nine-hole course set within a race track while the Al Ghazal Golf Club at Abu Dhabi International Airport has an 18-hole sand course and a golfing academy and hosts the annual World Sand Golf Championship. In Al Ain, golfers can try the nine-hole grass course at the Hilton International, where a putting green is also available, while a new course is being built in the Al Maqam district.

All the golf clubs are open to non-members and have driving ranges and golf academies with coaching provided by resident professionals. Their facilities include health clubs, swimming pools, tennis and snooker, as well as a range of eating and drinking options from casual sports bars to fine restaurants.

According to Sheikh Sultan bin Tahnoun Al Nahyan, Chairman of the Abu Dhabi Tourism Authority (ADTA), the tourism and leisure sector of Abu Dhabi is poised to seize a slice of the US$17.5 billion (Dhs 65 billion) global industry in golf tourism with new courses planned and the worldwide attention attracted by the Abu Dhabi Golf Championship, a European Tour-sanctioned event held at the Abu Dhabi Golf Club by Sheraton.

ADTA, which seeks to attract up to three million visitors a year to Abu Dhabi by 2015 – triple the current annual average – has identified golf tourism as a key growth area. While the championship draws spectators from overseas, it's the awareness the event creates among the global golfing community through the media that's expected to boost golf tourism in Abu Dhabi. Some 17,500 spectators follow the stars round the National Course, but live TV coverage reaches more than 120 million homes in 28 countries, and millions more viewers via recorded highlights on news and sports bulletins.

The development of two new courses on the 27 square kilometre Saadiyat Island (Island of Happiness) project, which is being developed in three phases, which started in 2006 and is projected to end in 2018, will further enhance the Emirate's appeal to golf tourists.

Whether you enjoy chess, quilting, birdwatching or classical music, there's also a full quota of social, cultural and natural-history clubs and societies. One of the most active is the Emirates Natural History Group, whose programme includes regular talks on local wildlife, geology and archaeology, as well as outings.

As the capital city, Abu Dhabi regularly attracts top international entertainers, from world-famous pop stars to ballet and opera companies. Many hotels also have nightclubs, each with their own character, serving different age groups and musical preferences. These include Western-style clubs playing up-to-the-minute music or, for a more traditional experience, there are also venues featuring Middle Eastern bands and belly dancers. International festivals range from Scandinavian promotions to a Rio Carnival, while the annual Al Ain Classical Music Festival attracts more and more music lovers every year.

The Abu Dhabi Cultural Foundation, part of the Abu Dhabi Authority for Culture and Heritage (ADACH), organizes an impressive variety of less-commercial events. Located in 14 hectares of lush gardens, this modern complex – designed in traditional Arabian style – stages a wide range of art exhibitions, concerts, plays, lectures, movie screenings, film festivals and poetry readings. Art workshops, language courses, children's activities and an annual book fair are also offered, while the National Library, with more than a million books, is also housed here.

Introducing the cultural life of the capital without mentioning its wonderful variety of restaurants would be unforgivable and, in Abu Dhabi, its hotel restaurants cater not only for their own guests but also for local residents, both UAE citizens and expatriates. There are dishes to satisfy all palates, including cuisines from round the world, seafood and themed buffets.

Just about every major international cuisine is represented, including restaurants where visitors can experience dishes of the Arab World – which include salads, fresh pastries, rice dishes and grilled meats – while enjoying the mood and traditions of local and regional dining.

In fact, visitors shouldn't hesitate to venture outside their hotels to sample the wide range of culinary experiences. Eating out is a great way to discover different areas and meet the cosmopolitan residents of Abu Dhabi. For a quieter evening, dinner on one of the floating dhow restaurants is sure to be a memorable choice.

Most of the familiar international fast-food chains are also found in Abu Dhabi and there are many small, good-value restaurants catering to local residents. Alcohol is served in hotel restaurants and bars to non-Muslims but, with a few exceptions, such as private clubs, is not available elsewhere.

Expect to find a 16 per cent service charge on top of the menu tariff in hotel restaurants. Although these taxes are incorporated into the customer's bill, an additional 10 per cent tip is appreciated by the attentive and friendly staff. An up-to-date listing of restaurants, cinemas, clubs, activities and contacts can be found each month in the Abu Dhabi edition of *What's On* magazine.

A Tour of Abu Dhabi City

Abu Dhabi's compact island location makes for easy navigation and it's a fascinating place to explore on foot or by taxi. Although a busy metropolis of spectacular high-rise towers, shopping malls, restaurants and hotels, interspersed with gracious residences, its layout reflects its origins as a fishing village. The city not only faces the Gulf, but many of the places of interest and hotels lie within five blocks of the sea.

With its walkways and greenery, the recently renovated and enlarged Corniche is the city's showpiece. You'll find people enjoying this beautiful area at any time of day – strolling or jogging along the waterfront or taking their families to one of the childrens' play areas or grassy parks.

At the western end of the Corniche is one of the newest and brightest jewels of Abu Dhabi's burgeoning tourism sector – the Emirates Palace Hotel. Adjacent to the hotel, a road leads to the Breakwater. Featuring the popular Marina Mall and the International Marine Sports Club, this area has a number of Arabian cafés and restaurants and a new marina and housing development are currently under construction. At sunset, the view from the end of the Breakwater to the Corniche and the tall buildings beyond is quite stunning.

Also on the Breakwater, the Heritage Village provides a taste of life before the oil era. Its displays offer an insight into Bedouin ways, as well as courtyard houses, windtowers and an example of the ancient *falaj* irrigation system used in the region's oases. In different workshops craftsmen and women demonstrate their skills and the museum has displays of garments, coins, Holy Qur'ans, diving equipment, jewellery and weaponry.

Between Khalidiya Street and Airport Road is Qasr al-Hosn, built in 1795 as the residence of the rulers of Abu Dhabi. Adjacent to it is the Cultural Foundation, home to the National Library, an auditorium, exhibition halls and a cinema. The Foundation is the hub of Abu Dhabi's cultural life, staging concerts, plays, lectures and other events. Traditional arts and crafts are practised at The Women's Craft Centre on Al Maktoum Street where the handiwork may be purchased.

Abu Dhabi has many other areas of interest to the visitor. Airport Road (officially Sheikh Rashid bin Saeed Al Maktoum Street), the spine of the city, is lined with shops, cafés and restaurants. On the western side of the island is Al Bateen, with several large parks and the Bateen dhow-building yard, where the ancient skill of dhow building can be observed, although this, sadly, is soon to be moved to another location so that the site can be developed. Al Safarat, at the eastern end of the island, houses the International Exhibition Centre, where major exhibitions are held.

In the port area east of the Corniche are the Al Meena, Iranian and Afghan souks, as well as fish, meat and vegetable markets; the fish souk is especially interesting. The nearby Dhow Harbour provides another fascinating taste of Abu Dhabi's living traditions set against a backdrop of towering skyscrapers.

The Dhow Harbour, set against a backdrop of towering skyscrapers, provides a fascinating taste of Abu Dhabi's living traditions.

Abu Dhabi – Garden City of the Gulf

Abu Dhabi – named the Garden City of the Gulf for good reason – has some 20 well-maintained parks, most of them with water features and children's play areas. The island is also well endowed with a number of golden beaches, some of which have been developed into beach parks.

Organized tours are a good way to see the attractions of Abu Dhabi and surrounding areas. These can be arranged through hotels or local tour operators. Taxis are plentiful and inexpensive while limos can be booked in advance. The Abu Dhabi Municipality operates a comprehensive and inexpensive network of bus routes and there's a regular 24-hour service linking Abu Dhabi International Airport and the city centre. The major car hire firms are all well represented in the cities and at the airports.

> Few tourists would deny harbouring a fascination with the falcon's regal appearance and its precision in hunting.

Abu Dhabi's hinterland

Also known as the Garden City, Al Ain was once a key oasis on the caravan route to Oman. Situated some 150 kilometres east of the capital, on an excellent highway, Al Ain boasts several historical forts and archaeological sites and fascinating insights into the city's origins can be found at the Al Ain Museum and the Natural History Museum at the Emirates University.

The Hili Archaeological Garden has the remains of a major Bronze Age settlement, with collective tombs, one of which contained more than 400 burials, and a large, fortified, mud-brick settlement, dating back more than 4,000 years. Jahili Fort, once home to the late ruler Sheikh Zayed, is notable for its main turret, with four levels, reminiscent of a wedding cake.

Al Ain is the most fertile region in the country and its many oases support a host of date-palm plantations and working farms. The city's many parks are all beautifully kept and add to its laid-back ambience. The Al Ain Zoo and Aquarium is one of the largest in the Gulf region. Recently refurbished, it is home to a wide variety of species, both common and rare, and runs an ongoing breeding programme for endangered species. Not to be missed, the city's camel market is the last of its kind in the UAE. Here you can see traders discussing prices and listing the merits of their prized camels.

Al Ain's Old Prison affords the best views of the city and its surrounding oases. Illuminated at night, this historical building offers a beautiful view when seen from the nearby camel market.

Overlooking the city is Jebel Hafeet, where a superb winding road leads to the summit, offering spectacular views in all directions. Scattered along its lower slopes are more ancient tombs, some as much as 5,000 years old. Situated nearly a kilometre above sea level, at the summit, is the Mercure Grand Jebel Hafeet hotel, while at the foot of the mountain are the Ain Al Faydah natural spring and the Green Mubazzarah tourism resort.

Some three hours by car from Abu Dhabi city is the Liwa Oasis, one of the largest oases on the Arabian Peninsula and the entry point to the famous Empty Quarter or Rub al-Khali. Featuring numerous date plantations, the oasis is home to the Bani Yas tribe, which is headed by Abu Dhabi's ruling family. The large tracts of desert, featuring some of the highest sand dunes in the world, have remained unchanged for centuries and stretch into Saudi Arabia, Oman and Yemen. The Empty Quarter has inspired explorers such as Sir Wilfred Thesiger and remains a firm favourite with today's leisure explorers – and all those with a love for wilderness areas.

Liwa is the base camp for the annual UAE Desert Challenge, which forms part of the international off-road rally world championships. Camel tours of Liwa's dunes and overnight camping trips are some of the options available through Abu Dhabi's many tour operators and the Liwa Hotel – an oasis in its own right.

Abu Dhabi – Garden City of the Gulf

Chapter Eight
The World on Display

Small neighbourhood souks are scattered throughout the city. They include the Afghani Souk, off Mina Road, that sells a variety of goods, including carpets.

Abu Dhabi offers an array of goods from all round the world, in shops that range from exclusive designer boutiques to open-air stalls. Shoppers in the city quickly discover an astonishing choice that combines the old and the new. There's the pleasure of exploring the malls, department stores, boutiques and souks, with the bonus of a superb variety of products and competitive prices – in fact, prices for many imported luxury goods are often cheaper than in their country of origin.

Traditional souks

The Middle Eastern souk, or market-place, has an ambience uniquely its own, reminiscent of another era. Traditionally, souks were a maze of shady alleyways but today many resemble a collection of small shops, although they still have the same buzz as their ancestors. Like voyagers of the past, today's travellers can still

The World on Display

find perfumes, jewellery, silks, spices, nuts and dried fruits beside cheap trinkets, plastic sandals and electronic toys.

Bargaining over prices is a time-honoured tradition throughout the souks of the Arab World and can be a way of practising your Arabic and improving your negotiating skills. With serious haggling, some prices can be halved . . . even walking away can be part of the bargaining process! The experience should be treated as fun and vendors appreciate a smile. However, once a price has been agreed upon, the customer is expected to buy. Many visitors remember this as a highlight of their trip. To avoid embarrassment, however, remember that in the plusher showrooms and boutiques, prices are usually fixed. Those taking their cameras along should note that it is always best to ask before taking somebody's photograph, and to avoid photographing women.

Smaller neighbourhood souks are scattered throughout the city, including one

The colourful Fish Souk adjacent to the Dhow Harbour is well worth visiting – both for its wonderful selection of local seafood and its colourful atmosphere.

87

Abu Dhabi – Garden City of the Gulf

arched pavilion off Mina Road, known as the Afghani Souk, that sells carpets, mattresses and pillows for the traditional *majlis* in addition to household goods. Apart from a few small hand-made rugs from Afghanistan, the carpets here are all machine-made, mass-produced copies of old patterns and styles and therefore reasonably priced. Bargaining is nonetheless recommended.

A little further away, at the Dhow Harbour, the Iranian Souk offers everything from plants, hand-painted tiles, terracotta pots, kilims and kitchenware to furniture. It is one of the most authentic souks in Abu Dhabi and worth a visit. The nearby fish market overflows with daily arrivals of local seafood, including shark and barracuda, and the open-air stalls of the fruit and vegetable souk bustle with shoppers and vendors auctioning crates of colourful produce.

Visitors to Abu Dhabi's souks often take home with them far more than their souvenirs – they take a lasting memory of local hospitality and atmosphere, and a time-honoured way of life that lives on even in today's modern society.

More conventional shopping can be found along and between the three main streets: Sheikh Zayed the Second, Sheikh Hamdan and Sheikh Khalifa, all running parallel to each other and to Abu Dhabi's scenic Corniche. The range of goods on offer is an eclectic combination of past and present.

For antique collectors, there are magnificent Arab chests, long the most prominent piece of traditional furniture in Gulf homes. Made of teak with solid brass handles, decorated with copper studs and ornate mother-of-pearl inlays, these genuine dowry chests, called *mendoos,* were traditionally presented to a girl by her father when she became engaged and were used for storing clothes and jewellery. Many have drawers in the bottom or secret compartments. Authentic antique *mendoos* are now eagerly sought and expensive.

A symbol of hospitality, copper and brass coffee pots, known in Arabic as *dalla,* are also indispensable to the Arab way of life, and have been for centuries. A small, strong cup of coffee is generally served after meals and to every visitor to your home or place of business. The coffee pot is an appropriate cultural emblem on the one dirham coin. Antique coffee pots are in great demand and can be found in a variety of styles depending on their region of origin, but all have the characteristic long, curved, beak-like spout. An old pot in reasonably good condition can command a high price.

Another popular traditional item is the *khanjar,* a short, curved steel dagger in a finely etched sheath that, until recently, was carried on a belt by every man in the region; old rifles, some decorated with silver inlays; falconry accoutrements such as hoods or decorative perches; and relics of the pearling industry – the curved knives used by the divers in the past are quite rare – as are the prized Gulf pearls that are still found from time to time in local shops.

Bedouin jewellery, typically heavy, chunky pieces in silver, often combined with semi-precious stones, is particularly striking. Bedouin women traditionally received their first set when they married: bracelets, necklaces, rings for fingers and toes, belts, earrings, medallions and amulets. The silver used in making these pieces used to be obtained by melting down Maria Theresa dollars, formerly the accepted currency throughout the Gulf. Those who buy several pieces of jewellery may also opt for an inlaid jewellery box and won't be disappointed with the selection available.

When budgets do not stretch to antiques, traditional wooden furniture, miniature dhows, or carpets, rugs and textiles from the region (including Iran, Pakistan, India and Afghanistan), there's a wide range of modest souvenirs and handicrafts to choose from, including prayer beads, *shisha* pipes, brass camels, trays, incense burners and the ubiquitous fridge magnet.

> Abu Dhabi Mall, with more than 200 upmarket shops and stalls, is situated in the Tourist Club area of the city.

Abu Dhabi – Garden City of the Gulf

Shoppers enjoy a quiet moment next to Marina Mall's impressive fountain. This modern shopping mall is situated on the Breakwater.

Modern shopping

The Emirate's malls, in both Abu Dhabi and Al Ain, are spacious, modern and imaginatively designed. Besides their fine array of shops and boutiques, including many famous international retail names, they have a good selection of food outlets and children's play areas. Sales and promotions run throughout the year and raffles are popular. The larger malls also house cinemas and have plenty of free parking.

With the arrival of Abu Dhabi's three newest and biggest malls, shopping in the capital attracts all the more attention. Located adjacent to the Beach Rotana Hotel in the Tourist Club area, the Abu Dhabi Mall is one of the largest in the UAE. The huge US$139 million (Dhs 510 million) complex, part of the Abu Dhabi Trade Centre, houses more than 200 shops and stores, and reflects Abu Dhabi's international standards with names such as Mont Blanc, Pierre Cardin, The Body Shop and Virgin Megastore.

Shoppers can find everything from affordable fashions and exclusive designer labels and accessories to gifts, jewellery, digital cameras, video equipment and music – and they're also treated to a fine selection of coffee shops and restaurants.

The Marina Mall, set at the Breakwater overlooking the capital's impressive skyline, promises a different shopping, entertainment and leisure experience. With its landmark rooftop, the recently expanded Marina Mall is a shopper's paradise, boasting major international chains such as Ikea and Carrefour as well as numerous shops and boutiques. It also features one of the largest multiplex cinemas in the UAE and a unique fountain that can emulate rain and fog, synchronized to the background music.

The latest arrival is the Al Wahda Mall, just off Airport Road (Sheikh Rashid bin Saeed Al Maktoum Street) in the centre of the city, again well-stocked with a wide variety of shops and cafés.

With mall shopping now well established in the city, these three are now set to face competition from others, the Khalidiyah Mall being just one of several seeking their share of the expanding business in the rapidly growing capital.

Gold is very competitively priced in Abu Dhabi and there are numerous jewellery shops around town. The Madinat Zayed Shopping and Gold Centre on 'Muroor' Road, not far from downtown Sheikh Hamdan Street, is another large city mall with its own special attractions. Divided into two huge but elegant buildings, each topped by three domes, it is a vast retail complex and gold centre. The latter is an excellent place to bargain for items of exquisite craftsmanship, sold by weight at prices much lower than in the West. The former is particularly well supplied with fabrics – sequinned gauzes, gold-threaded brocades, iridescent silks from Japan, raw silks from India and flowery organdies in rich glowing tones, delicate pastels and shimmering golds and silvers.

Other malls include Liwa Centre, Al Hana Shopping Centre, Al Muhairy Centre, Fatouh Al Khair, Hamdan Centre, Khalifa Centre, Rotana Mall, Abu Dhabi Co-operative Society and Lamcy Plaza. Al Ain also has some excellent shopping facilities, notably Al Ain Mall and Al Jimi Mall.

For those after gift shops, there are a number in Abu Dhabi selling exquisite crystal, silver, leather goods, china and porcelain figurines imported from all over the world. Lalique, Bernardaud, Daum, Baccarat, Limoges, Dupont and Christofle are some of the famous European names for glassware, crystal and China in the capital's more exclusive boutiques.

Designer clothes for women and men are not in short supply either: Yves Saint Laurent and Dior from Paris; Hugo Boss from Germany; Giorgio Armani from Italy; and Ralph Lauren from America – to name a few – can be found around town in the various luxury boutiques. Lower priced fashion stores such as Benetton, British

The World on Display

Abu Dhabi – Garden City of the Gulf

Abu Dhabi Duty Free, one of the best in the world, is recognized for the quality of its marketing efforts and its innovation.

Home Stores, Marks & Spencer and Next operate under franchises, and there are scores of shops selling cotton casuals from the Indian subcontinent.

Art shops often sell prints, watercolours or pen-and-ink drawings of local scenes, many painted by expatriate artists who have been inspired by the heritage, landscape and wildlife of the Emirates. On a practical level, it is worth pointing out that the local pharmacies are well stocked with the latest pharmaceutical products, as well as toiletries and cosmetics.

Local supermarkets, such as Spinneys, also offer a huge selection of international foods, whether Oreo cookies, Chinese noodles, Russian caviar, French brie, Australian fruit or South African biltong, in order to satisfy an eclectic international expatriate community. For those with a sweet tooth, pastries in this part of the world may prove irresistible. Arab sweets, made with honey or syrup, stuffed with dates, sprinkled with crushed pistachio nuts, and soaked in rose water, are delicious, especially when accompanied by a traditional glass of tea with mint leaves.

Muffins, croissants, French pastries and nut breads are commonly sold around town in established outlets such as Café du Roi, Starbucks, La Brioche and other such coffee shops.

The World on Display

Duty free shopping

No account of Abu Dhabi's elaborate shopping facilities would be complete without mention of the award-winning duty-free complex at Abu Dhabi International Airport. Located in the airport's state-of-the-art satellite terminal, its branded shops and corners are spread across more than 5,000 square metres of retail space. Better known as ADDF, it opened its doors in 1984, has grown into one of the best duty-free complexes in the world and is internationally recognized for its marketing, quality and innovation.

Set in a domed concourse decorated with striking Arabian-style hexagonal tiling, its prices are competitive and customer service is of a high standard. ADDF pioneered the shop-in-shop concept with branded corners for international brands displaying their corporate identities. Prestigious brand names in fashion, fragrance, cosmetics, confectionery and more create an opulent look and feel to the retail area and there are separate departments for electronic items, local antiques and souvenirs, perfumes, fashion, food, books, watches, jewellery, tobacco, liquor and toys. Necessities such as pharmaceuticals and toiletries are also available. The complex is also famous for its 'Big Ticket' and other promotions that can turn a lucky ticket holder into the owner of a million dirhams or a luxury car.

Abu Dhabi – Garden City of the Gulf

Selected hotels in Abu Dhabi

Abu Dhabi's many fine hotels – a number of them overlooking the Arabian Gulf – rank among the best in the world, with renowed international and local brands ensuring the highest standards and facilities for the visitor. The local market expects first-class international service and the Emirate's leading hotels are geared to meet the most exacting standards. A selection of drop hotels follows . . .

Hotels

Al Diar Mina Hotel
PO Box 44421, Abu Dhabi, UAE
Tel: (+971 2) 678 1000 Fax: (+971 2) 679 1000
Email: minahotelre@gency-mina.ae   www.aldiarhotels.com

The Al Diar Mina Hotel combines the ambience of casual homeliness with the complete services of a furnished business hotel at an excellent price. Ideally located along Al Meena Street, within the city centre, the hotel is less than half an hour's drive from the International Airport and provides easy access to the business and commercial centres of Abu Dhabi. The hotel offers spacious and elegantly appointed guest rooms and suites, with spectacular views of the city, along with complete room amenities, facilities and services. With a comfortable and relaxed atmosphere, combined with warm and friendly service, a stay at the Al Diar Mina Hotel guarantees great value for money.

Al Diar Regency Hotel
PO Box 47600, Abu Dhabi, UAE
Tel: (+971 2) 676 5000 Fax: (+971 2) 677 7446
Email: reservation@regency-mina.ae   www.aldiarhotels.com

The recently refurbished Al Diar Regency Hotel, is conveniently located in the city centre along the scenic Abu Dhabi Corniche, within the city's commercial and business district. Offering spectacular views of the Arabian Gulf and the dramatic city skyline, this business hotel boasts well-appointed guest rooms and suites with modern and stylish décor, full room amenities and a wide range of facilities and services. The hotel's main restaurant, The Regent's Court, serves delectable international cuisine in a cozy atmosphere with stunning views of the Arabian Gulf. The hotel has bars for entertainment and a well-equipped health club. With its full range of facilities and services, combined with the attentive and friendly service, guests are assured of a pleasant stay at the Al Diar Regency Hotel.

Al Raha Beach Hotel
PO Box 38616, Abu Dhabi, UAE
Tel: (+971 2) 508 0472   Fax: (+971 2) 508 0428
Email: reservation@danatresortalraha.ae   www.danahotelgroup.com

A short drive from the airport and city, the hotel is set in stunning, landscaped gardens and overlooks wide, sandy white beaches with magnificent views of the Arabian Gulf. The 110 deluxe rooms and suites, including four executive, two diplomatic and five royal suites have been hailed as 'the most spacious and elegantly appointed' in the region. The hotel boasts a unique and stylish décor, comfort, superb amenities and a dedicated team which provide guests with an unparalleled level of service. For guests seeking additional exclusi-vity and privacy, there are also 24 two, three and four bedroom luxury villas offering a perfect alternative for those seeking five-star hotel services in the privacy of their own home. The villas and their surrounding areas provide seclu-sion and privacy with their own clubhouse and outdoor swimming pool and beach.

Beach Rotana Abu Dhabi
PO Box 45200, Abu Dhabi, UAE
Tel: (+971 2) 644 3000   Fax: (+971 2) 644 2111
Email: res.beach@rotana.com   www.rotana.com

Ideally located in the heart of the capital's business and shopping districts, the Beach Rotana is set on its own stretch of pristine white beach in the Tourist Club area, just thirty minutes away from Abu Dhabi International Airport. Intimate corridors usher you into 413 sea-facing guest rooms and suites, including eight dedicated Club Rotana Floors and two Royal Suites. Our ten world-class restaurants entice you to savour flavours from around the world while keeping fit and relaxed with our private beach, temperature-controlled swimming pools, Bodylines - fitness centre, PADI dive center and Zen the Spa.

Abu Dhabi – Garden City of the Gulf

Crowne Plaza Abu Dhabi
PO Box 3541, Abu Dhabi, UAE
Tel: (+971 2) 616 2222 Fax: (+971 2) 633 1340
Email: reservations@cpabudhabi.ae www.crowneplaza.com/abudhabiuab

Crowne Plaza Abu Dhabi is a five-star hotel conveniently located in the city centre, minutes away from key business locations. The hotel provides friendly, personalized service and a range of facilities from wi-fi access throughout the hotel, to complimentary shuttle bus services. Crowne Plaza Abu Dhabi's luxurious rooms are spacious and provide, in addition to wi-fi, cabled high-speed internet access. The hotel offers an excellent choice of international restaurants and bars. For holiday makers, there are competititve prices and facilities. The eighteen-metre long roof-top pool provides skyline views and an opportunity to exercise or relax. Other facilities include a well-equipped fitness centre, massage services, steam and sauna, and a whirlpool overlooking the city.

InterContinental Abu Dhabi
PO Box 4171, Abu Dhabi, UAE
Tel: (+971 2) 666 6888 Fax: (+971 2) 666 9153
Email: abudhabi@icauh.ae www.intercontinental.com

The InterContinental Abu Dhabi boasts understated, elegant deluxe and executive guest rooms and a variety of suites all the way up to the Presidential and Royal suites. In addition, breathtaking views over the city skyline, Corniche and coastline make this the place to see the city at its best. The picturesque marina provides a focal point for the finest restaurants in town, showcasing the best in Brazilian, Italian and fresh seafood, combined with exciting live entertainment. The Health Club offers 285 metres of private white sandy beach in addition to the Health Zone with a fully equipped gym and wellness facilities. The hotel is also a modern, contemporary venue for hosting the most special of events, with a focus on personal service and attention to detail at all times.

Le Royal Meridien
PO Box 45505, Abu Dhabi, UAE
Tel: (+971 2) 674 2020   Fax: (+971 2) 695 0434
Email: reservations.lrmad@lemeridien.com
www.Leroyalmeridienabudhabi.com

Le Royal Meridien Abu Dhabi is the contemporary international business destination. Discover stimulating sea and city views from our 276 rooms and suites designed for the forward-thinking, modern corporate guest. The hotel, in the heart of the business district, is situated just thirty minutes from the Abu Dhabi International Airport and offers a multitude of room amenities to ensure a pleasurable stay for any guest. With twelve outlets to choose from, our guests can engage their palettes in a sophisticated culinary dining experience, ranging from the iconic Al Fanar, the only revolving rooftop restaurant in the city, to the Shuja Yacht, where guests enjoy an illuminating view of the Abu Dhabi city skyline, while uncovering the savoury tastes of the sea.

One to One Hotel – The Village
PO Box 46689, Abu Dhabi, UAE
Tel: (+971 2) 495 2020 Fax: (+971 2) 495 2001
Email: res.thevillage@onetoonehotels.com www.onetoonehotels.com

A distinctive new addition to Abu Dhabi's leisure industry, this 128-room hotel has been designed with both the business and leisure traveller in mind. It hosts a unique selection of guest rooms and suites, housed in 18 subtle clusters, each with its own rooftop pool. Stylish décor and an informal ambience combine to deliver a residential experience that is incomparable, and features the highest levels of service and attention to detail. One to One Hotel – The Village is centrally located within Abu Dhabi, just off Al Salam Street. An exciting new business hub and development, it is within easy reach of Abu Dhabi's commercial centre and is conveniently accessible from all business, commercial and major attractions.